Contents

Nonfiction Reading Practice Is Important

Research indicates that more than 80 percent of what people read and write is nonfiction text. Newspapers, magazines, directions on new products, application forms, and how-to manuals are just some of the types of nonfiction reading material we encounter on a daily basis. As students move through the grades, an increasing amount of time is spent reading expository text for subjects such as science and social studies. Most reading comprehension sections on state and national tests are nonfiction.

Each Unit Has...

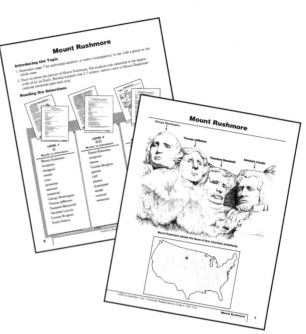

A Teacher Resource Page

Vocabulary words for all three levels are given. The vocabulary lists include proper nouns and content-specific terms, as well as other challenging words.

A Visual Aid

The visual aid represents the topic for the unit. It is intended to build interest in the topic. Reproduce the visual on an overhead transparency or photocopy it for each student.

Articles at Three Reading Levels

Each unit presents three articles on the same topic. The articles progress in difficulty from easiest (Level 1) to hardest (Level 3). An icon indicates the level of the article—Level 1 (■), Level 2 (■ ■), Level 3 (■ ■ ■). Each article contains new vocabulary and ideas to incorporate into classroom discussion. The Level 1 article gives readers a core vocabulary and a basic understanding of the topic. More challenging vocabulary words are used as the level of the article increases. Interesting details also change or increase in the Levels 2 and 3 articles.

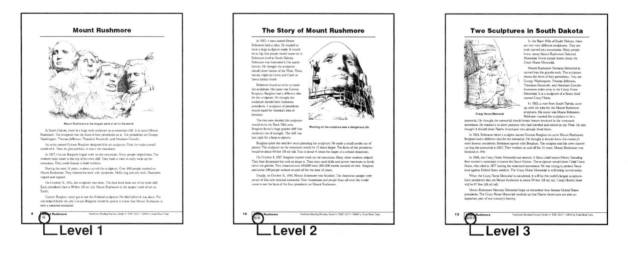

Level 1   Level 2   Level 3

Readability

All of the articles in this series have been edited for readability. Readability formulas, which are mathematical calculations, are considered to be one way of predicting reading ease. The Flesch-Kincaid and Fry Graph formulas were used to check for readability. These formulas count and factor in three variables: the number of words, syllables, and sentences in a passage to determine the reading level. When appropriate, proper nouns and content-specific terms were discounted in determining readability levels for the articles in this book.

Nonfiction Reading Practice, Grade 4 • EMC 3315 • ©2003 by Evan-Moor Corp.

Student Comprehension Pages

A vocabulary/comprehension page follows each article. There are five multiple-choice questions that provide practice with the types of questions that are generally used on standardized reading tests. The bonus question is intended to elicit higher-level thinking skills.

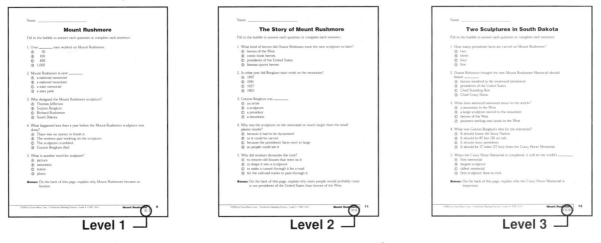

Level 1 ⌐   Level 2 ⌐   Level 3 ⌐

Additional Resources

Six graphic organizers to extend comprehension are also included in the book. (See page 4 for suggested uses.)

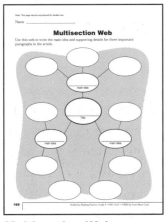

Biography Sketch

KWL Chart

Making an Outline

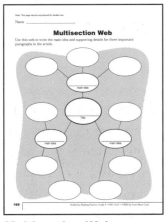

Multisection Web

Sequence Chart

Vocabulary Quilt

How to Use *Nonfiction Reading Practice*

Planning Guided Reading Instruction

The units in this book do not need to be taught in sequential order. Choose the units that align with your curriculum or with student interests.

- For whole-group instruction, introduce the unit to the total class. Provide each student with an article at the appropriate reading level. Guide students as they read the articles. You may want to have students read with partners. Then conduct a class discussion to share the different information learned.

- For small-group instruction, choose an article at the appropriate reading level for each group. The group reads the article with teacher guidance and discusses the information presented.

- The articles may also be used to assist readers in moving from less difficult to more challenging reading material. After building vocabulary and familiarity with the topic at the appropriate level, students may be able to successfully read the article at the next level of difficulty.

Presenting a Unit

1. Before reading the articles, make an overhead transparency of the visual aid or reproduce it for individual student use. Use the visual to engage student interest in the topic, present vocabulary, and build background that will aid in comprehension. This step is especially important for visual learners.

2. Present vocabulary that may be difficult to decode or understand. A list of suggested vocabulary words for each article is given on the teacher resource page. Where possible, connect these words to the visual aid.

3. Present and model several appropriate reading strategies that aid in comprehension of the expository text. You may wish to make an overhead transparency of the reading strategies checklist on page 5 or reproduce it for students to refer to as they read.

4. You may want to use one of the graphic organizers provided on pages 166–171. Make an overhead transparency, copy the organizer onto the board or chart paper, or reproduce it for students. Record information learned to help students process and organize the information.

5. Depending on the ability levels of the students, the comprehension/vocabulary pages may be completed as a group or as independent practice. It is always advantageous to share and discuss answers as a group so that students correct misconceptions. An answer key is provided at the back of this book.

Nonfiction Reading Practice, Grade 4 • EMC 3315 • ©2003 by Evan-Moor Corp.

Reading Checklist

Directions: Check off the reading hints that you use to understand the story.

Before I Read

_____ I think about what I already know.

_____ I think about what I want to learn.

_____ I predict what is going to happen.

_____ I read the title for clues.

_____ I look at the pictures and read the captions for extra clues.

_____ I skim the article to read headings and words in bold or italic print.

_____ I read over the comprehension questions for the article.

While I Read

_____ I ask questions and read for answers.

_____ I reread parts that are confusing.

_____ I reread the captions under the pictures.

_____ I make mental pictures as I read.

_____ I use context clues to understand difficult words.

_____ I take notes when I am reading.

_____ I underline important key words and phrases.

After I Read

_____ I think about what I have just read.

_____ I speak, draw, and write about what I read.

_____ I confirm or change the predictions I made.

_____ I reread to find the main idea.

_____ I reread to find details.

_____ I read the notes I took as I read.

_____ I look back at the article to find answers to questions.

Mount Rushmore

Introducing the Topic

1. Reproduce page 7 for individual students, or make a transparency to use with a group or the whole class.

2. Show students the picture of Mount Rushmore. Tell students this memorial is the largest work of art on Earth. Then show students the map of the United States and where Mount Rushmore is located. Tell students that 2.5 million visitors come to Mount Rushmore National Memorial each year.

Reading the Selections

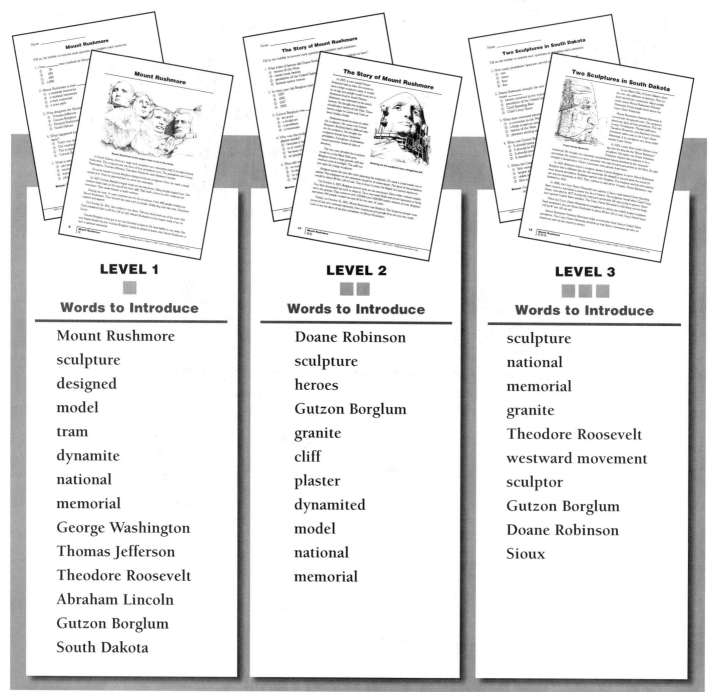

LEVEL 1
Words to Introduce

Mount Rushmore

sculpture

designed

model

tram

dynamite

national

memorial

George Washington

Thomas Jefferson

Theodore Roosevelt

Abraham Lincoln

Gutzon Borglum

South Dakota

LEVEL 2
Words to Introduce

Doane Robinson

sculpture

heroes

Gutzon Borglum

granite

cliff

plaster

dynamited

model

national

memorial

LEVEL 3
Words to Introduce

sculpture

national

memorial

granite

Theodore Roosevelt

westward movement

sculptor

Gutzon Borglum

Doane Robinson

Sioux

Nonfiction Reading Practice, Grade 4 • EMC 3315 • ©2003 by Evan-Moor Corp.

Mount Rushmore

George Washington

Thomas Jefferson

Theodore Roosevelt

Abraham Lincoln

Mount Rushmore shows the faces of four American presidents.

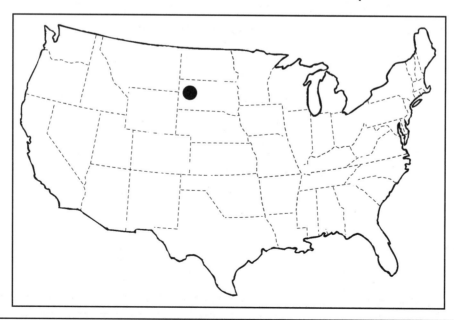

Mount Rushmore

Mount Rushmore is the largest work of art in the world.

In South Dakota, there is a huge rock sculpture on a mountain cliff. It is called Mount Rushmore. The sculpture has the faces of four presidents on it. The presidents are George Washington, Thomas Jefferson, Theodore Roosevelt, and Abraham Lincoln.

An artist named Gutzon Borglum designed this art sculpture. First, he made a small model of it. Then he planned how to carve the mountain.

In 1927, Gutzon Borglum began work on the mountain. Many people helped him. The workers built stairs to the top of the rock cliff. They built a tram to carry tools up the mountain. They made frames to hold workers.

During the next 14 years, workers carved the sculpture. Over 400 men worked on Mount Rushmore. They blasted the rock with dynamite. Drills dug into the rock. Hammers tapped and tapped.

On October 31, 1941, the sculpture was done. The four faces look out of the rock cliff. Each president's face is 60 feet (18 m) tall. Mount Rushmore is the largest work of art on Earth.

Gutzon Borglum never got to see the finished sculpture. He died less than a year before it was done. His son helped finish the job. Gutzon Borglum would be proud to know that Mount Rushmore is now a national memorial.

Nonfiction Reading Practice, Grade 4 • EMC 3315 • ©2003 by Evan-Moor Corp.

Name _____

Mount Rushmore

Fill in the bubble to answer each question or complete each sentence.

1. Over _____ men worked on Mount Rushmore.
   - Ⓐ   50
   - Ⓑ   100
   - Ⓒ   400
   - Ⓓ 1,000

2. Mount Rushmore is now _____.
   - Ⓐ a national memorial
   - Ⓑ a national mountain
   - Ⓒ a state memorial
   - Ⓓ a state park

3. Who designed the Mount Rushmore sculpture?
   - Ⓐ Thomas Jefferson
   - Ⓑ Gutzon Borglum
   - Ⓒ Richard Rushmore
   - Ⓓ South Dakota

4. What happened less than a year before the Mount Rushmore sculpture was done?
   - Ⓐ There was no money to finish it.
   - Ⓑ The workers quit working on the sculpture.
   - Ⓒ The sculpture crumbled.
   - Ⓓ Gutzon Borglum died.

5. What is another word for *sculpture*?
   - Ⓐ picture
   - Ⓑ mountain
   - Ⓒ statue
   - Ⓓ photo

Bonus: On the back of this page, explain why Mount Rushmore became so famous.

The Story of Mount Rushmore

In 1923, a man named Doane Robinson had an idea. He wanted to have a large sculpture made. It would be so big that people would come see it. Robinson lived in South Dakota. Robinson was interested in his state's history. He thought the sculpture should show heroes of the West. These heroes might be Lewis and Clark or Sioux Indian chiefs.

Robinson found an artist to make the sculpture. His name was Gutzon Borglum. Borglum had a different idea for the sculpture. He thought the sculpture should have American presidents. A sculpture of presidents would stand for America's idea of freedom.

The two men decided the sculpture would be in the Black Hills area. Borglum found a huge granite cliff that received a lot of sunlight. The cliff was just right for a large sculpture.

Working on the sculpture was a dangerous job.

Borglum spent the next few years planning his sculpture. He made a small model out of plaster. The sculpture on the mountain would be 12 times larger. The faces of the presidents would be about 60 feet (18 m) tall. That is about 6 times the height of a school classroom.

On October 4, 1927, Borglum started work on the mountain. Many other workers helped. They first dynamited the rock to shape it. Then they used drills and power hammers to finely carve the granite. They removed over 450,000 tons (405,000 metric tonnes) of rock. Borglum and about 400 people worked on and off for the next 14 years.

Finally, on October 31, 1941, Mount Rushmore was finished. The American people were proud of this new national memorial. Now Americans and people from all over the world come to see the faces of the four presidents on Mount Rushmore.

Name _____

The Story of Mount Rushmore

Fill in the bubble to answer each question or complete each sentence.

1. What kind of heroes did Doane Robinson want the new sculpture to have?
   - Ⓐ heroes of the West
   - Ⓑ comic book heroes
   - Ⓒ presidents of the United States
   - Ⓓ famous sports heroes

2. In what year did Borglum start work on the mountain?
   - Ⓐ 1997
   - Ⓑ 1941
   - Ⓒ 1927
   - Ⓓ 1903

3. Gutzon Borglum was _____.
   - Ⓐ an artist
   - Ⓑ a sculpture
   - Ⓒ a president
   - Ⓓ a mountain

4. Why was the sculpture on the mountain so much larger than the small plaster model?
   - Ⓐ because it had to be dynamited
   - Ⓑ so it could be carved
   - Ⓒ because the presidents' faces were so large
   - Ⓓ so people could see it

5. Why did workers dynamite the rock?
   - Ⓐ to remove old houses that were on it
   - Ⓑ to help shape it into a sculpture
   - Ⓒ to make a tunnel through it for a road
   - Ⓓ for the railroad tracks to pass through it

Bonus: On the back of this page, explain why more people might come to see presidents of the United States rather than heroes of the West.

Two Sculptures in South Dakota

Crazy Horse Memorial

In the Black Hills of South Dakota, there are two very different sculptures. They are both carved into mountains. Many people know about Mount Rushmore National Memorial. Fewer people know about the Crazy Horse Memorial.

Mount Rushmore National Memorial is carved into the granite rock. The sculpture shows the faces of four presidents. They are George Washington, Thomas Jefferson, Theodore Roosevelt, and Abraham Lincoln. Seventeen miles away is the Crazy Horse Memorial. It is a sculpture of a Sioux chief named Crazy Horse.

In 1923, a man from South Dakota came up with the idea for the Mount Rushmore sculpture. His name was Doane Robinson. Robinson wanted the sculpture to be a memorial. He thought the memorial should honor heroes involved in the westward movement. He wanted it to show pioneers who had traveled and settled in the West. He also thought it should show Native Americans who already lived there.

In 1924, Robinson hired a sculptor named Gutzon Borglum to carve Mount Rushmore. Borglum had a different idea for the memorial. He thought it should show the country's most famous presidents. Robinson agreed with Borglum. The sculptor and his crew started carving the memorial in 1927. They worked on and off for 14 years. Mount Rushmore was finished in 1941.

In 1948, the Crazy Horse Memorial was started. A Sioux chief named Henry Standing Bear wanted a memorial to honor the Sioux Nation. The sculpture would show Chief Crazy Horse, who died in 1877 during the westward movement. He was trying to protect Sioux land against United States soldiers. The Crazy Horse Memorial is still being carved today.

When the Crazy Horse Memorial is completed, it will be the world's largest sculpture. Each president's face on Mount Rushmore is about 60 feet (18 m) tall. Crazy Horse's head will be 87 feet (26 m) tall.

Mount Rushmore National Memorial helps us remember four famous United States presidents. The Crazy Horse Memorial will remind us that Native Americans are also an important part of our country's history.

Name _____

Two Sculptures in South Dakota

Fill in the bubble to answer each question or complete each sentence.

1. How many presidents' faces are carved on Mount Rushmore?
   Ⓐ two
   Ⓑ three
   Ⓒ four
   Ⓓ five

2. Doane Robinson thought the new Mount Rushmore Memorial should honor _____.
   Ⓐ heroes involved in the westward movement
   Ⓑ presidents of the United States
   Ⓒ Chief Standing Bear
   Ⓓ Chief Crazy Horse

3. What does *westward movement* mean in the article?
   Ⓐ a mountain in the West
   Ⓑ a large sculpture moved to the mountain
   Ⓒ heroes of the West
   Ⓓ pioneers settling onto lands in the West

4. What was Gutzon Borglum's idea for the memorial?
   Ⓐ It should honor the Sioux Nation.
   Ⓑ It should be 87 feet (26 m) tall.
   Ⓒ It should show presidents.
   Ⓓ It should be 17 miles (27 km) from the Crazy Horse Memorial.

5. When the Crazy Horse Memorial is completed, it will be the world's _____.
   Ⓐ first memorial
   Ⓑ largest sculpture
   Ⓒ oldest memorial
   Ⓓ first sculpture done in rock

Bonus: On the back of this page, explain why the Crazy Horse Memorial is important.

The United States Congress

Introducing the Topic

1. Reproduce page 15 for individual students, or make a transparency to use with a group or the whole class.

2. Show students the picture of the Capitol Building. Tell students the Capitol is where the Congress (Senate and House of Representatives) meets. Explain that it is located in Washington, D.C., our nation's capital. Then show the diagram of the Capitol and point out where the Senate and House of Representatives work.

Reading the Selections

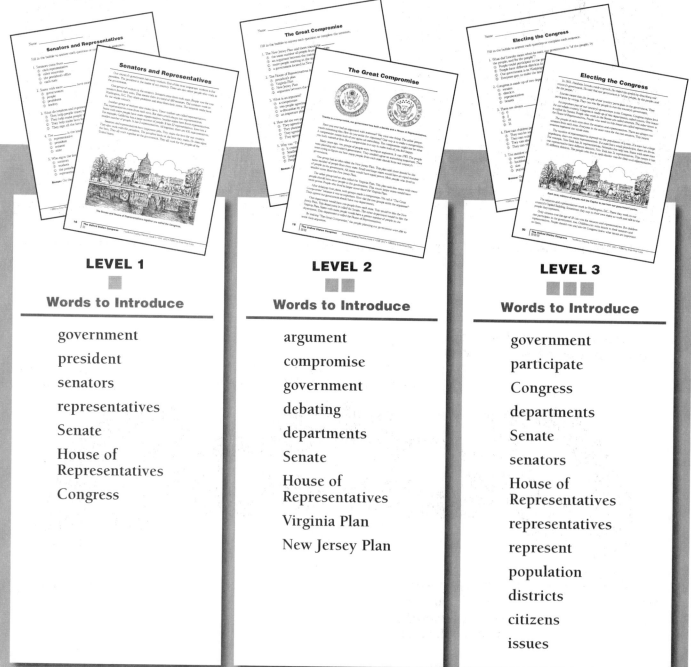

LEVEL 1

Words to Introduce

- government
- president
- senators
- representatives
- Senate
- House of Representatives
- Congress

LEVEL 2

Words to Introduce

- argument
- compromise
- government
- debating
- departments
- Senate
- House of Representatives
- Virginia Plan
- New Jersey Plan

LEVEL 3

Words to Introduce

- government
- participate
- Congress
- departments
- Senate
- senators
- House of Representatives
- representatives
- represent
- population
- districts
- citizens
- issues

Nonfiction Reading Practice, Grade 4 • EMC 3315 • ©2003 by Evan-Moor Corp.

The Capitol Building

The Senate and the House of Representatives are located in the Capitol Building in Washington, D.C.

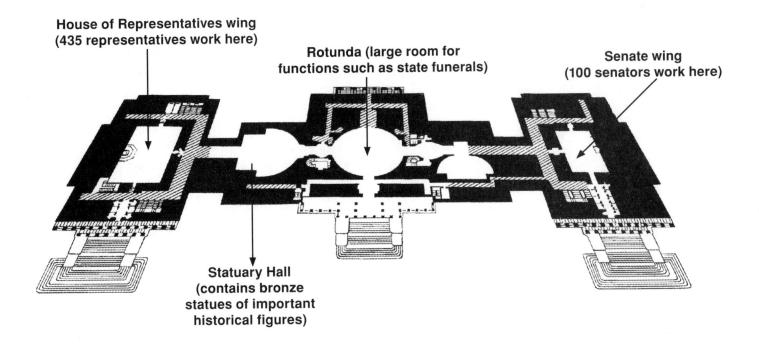

House of Representatives wing
(435 representatives work here)

Rotunda (large room for
functions such as state funerals)

Senate wing
(100 senators work here)

Statuary Hall
(contains bronze
statues of important
historical figures)

Senators and Representatives

Our country's government has many workers. One of the most important workers is the president. The president is the leader of our country. There are also other people who work in the government.

One group of workers is the senators. Senators come from each state. People vote for two senators from their state. That means there is a total of 100 senators. The senators work in Washington, D.C. They share problems and ideas from their states. The senators make laws for the whole country.

Another group of workers also makes laws. These workers are called representatives. The representatives come from each state. But there aren't always two representatives. States with more people have more representatives. Smaller states have fewer representatives. For example, California has a large number of people. It has 52 representatives. Iowa has a smaller number of people. It has 2 representatives. All together, there are 435 representatives.

Senators and representatives have important jobs. They make the laws for our country. They also work with the president. The president looks at the laws they make. He then signs the laws. They all work together in the government. They all work for the people of the United States.

The Senate and House of Representatives together are called the Congress.

Senators and Representatives

Fill in the bubble to answer each question or complete each sentence.

1. Senators come from _____.
   - Ⓐ each representative
   - Ⓑ other countries
   - Ⓒ the president's office
   - Ⓓ each state

2. States with more _____ have more representatives.
   - Ⓐ governments
   - Ⓑ people
   - Ⓒ presidents
   - Ⓓ leaders

3. What do senators and representatives do to help the country?
   - Ⓐ They help people travel to Washington, D.C.
   - Ⓑ They help make people want to move to our country.
   - Ⓒ They help make laws for the whole country.
   - Ⓓ They sign all the laws.

4. The _____ is the leader of our country.
   - Ⓐ representative
   - Ⓑ president
   - Ⓒ senator
   - Ⓓ state

5. Who signs the laws?
   - Ⓐ senators
   - Ⓑ workers
   - Ⓒ the president
   - Ⓓ representatives

Bonus: On the back of this page, explain why we have 100 senators.

The Great Compromise

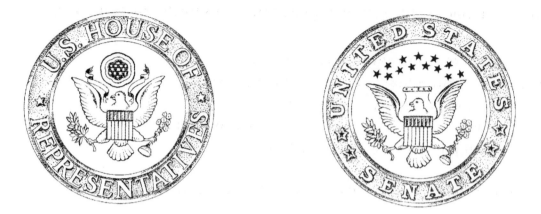

Thanks to a compromise, our government has both a Senate and a House of Representatives.

Have you ever had an argument with someone? You want one thing. The other person wants something else. How do you settle the argument? One way is to make a compromise. A compromise means both of you agree on something. The compromise might not be what you both wanted at first. But a compromise is a way to make both of you feel happy.

Many years ago, two groups of people were having an argument. It was 1787. The people were planning our country's government. They couldn't agree on something important. They were trying to figure out how many people from each state should form our country's government.

One group had an idea called the New Jersey Plan. This plan said there should be the same number of people from every state. Small and large states would have an equal number of people in the government. All states would have equal power. Most people who lived in smaller states liked the New Jersey Plan.

The other group had an idea called the Virginia Plan. This plan said that states with more people should have more people in the government. This meant larger states would have more power. People who lived in larger states liked the Virginia Plan.

After debating their plans, both groups made a compromise. We call it "The Great Compromise" because it was so important. How did the two groups settle the argument? They agreed our government should have two departments.

One department would have two people from each state. This would be like the New Jersey Plan. This department is called the Senate. The other department would be like the Virginia Plan. States with more people would have a greater number of people in the department. This department is called the House of Representatives.

By making "The Great Compromise," the people planning our government were able to settle their argument.

Name _____

The Great Compromise

Fill in the bubble to answer each question or complete the sentence.

1. The New Jersey Plan said there should be _____.
   - Ⓐ the same number of people from every state
   - Ⓑ an argument between the states
   - Ⓒ more people working in the state governments
   - Ⓓ a government located in New Jersey

2. The House of Representatives is like the _____.
   - Ⓐ president's plan
   - Ⓑ Virginia Plan
   - Ⓒ New Jersey Plan
   - Ⓓ argument between the states

3. What is an *argument*?
   - Ⓐ a compromise
   - Ⓑ two people agreeing on the same thing
   - Ⓒ a discussion by people who disagree
   - Ⓓ an important plan

4. How did the two groups settle their argument?
   - Ⓐ They agreed on the New Jersey Plan.
   - Ⓑ They planned to have one department.
   - Ⓒ They agreed on the Virginia Plan.
   - Ⓓ They agreed our government should have two departments.

5. Why was "The Great Compromise" so important?
   - Ⓐ It created the Senate and the House of Representatives.
   - Ⓑ Smaller states had more power in the government.
   - Ⓒ Larger states had more power in the government.
   - Ⓓ People never argued again.

Bonus: On the back of this page, explain why "The Great Compromise" was fair.

Electing the Congress

In 1863, Abraham Lincoln made a speech. He ended his speech by describing our country's government. He said that our government is "of the people, by the people, and for the people."

Lincoln meant that the people of our country participate in the government. They participate by voting. They can vote for people to run the country's government.

An important part of our country's government is the Congress. Congress makes laws for our whole country. Congress is made up of two departments, called houses. One house is called the Senate. People who work in the Senate are called senators. The other house is the House of Representatives. People who work in this house are called representatives.

The people of each state elect the senators and representatives. There are always two senators from each state. Everyone in the state votes for the two senators. This means senators represent the whole state.

The number of representatives depends on the population of a state. If a state has a large population, there are many representatives. If a state has a small population, there are fewer. For example, New York has 31 representatives. Nebraska has only one. States with more than one representative have different districts. New York has 31 representatives. This means it has 31 different districts. The people who live in each district vote for their own representative.

Each year, millions of people visit the Capitol to see how our government works.

The senators and representatives work in Washington, D.C. There they work in our country's Capitol Building. Sometimes they stay in their own states to work and talk to the people they represent.

Only citizens over the age of 18 can vote for senators and representatives. But children can participate in the government, too. Children can write letters to their senators and representatives. People should vote and also let Congress know what issues are important to them.

Name _____

Electing the Congress

Fill in the bubble to answer each question or complete each sentence.

1. What did Lincoln mean when he said our government is "of the people, by the people, and for the people"?
   Ⓐ People could participate in the government.
   Ⓑ People have different districts in the government.
   Ⓒ Our government is in Washington, D.C.
   Ⓓ Everyone gets to make the laws.

2. Congress is made up of two departments. They are called _____.
   Ⓐ senates
   Ⓑ districts
   Ⓒ representatives
   Ⓓ houses

3. There are always _____ senators from each state.
   Ⓐ 0
   Ⓑ 2
   Ⓒ 18
   Ⓓ 31

4. How can children participate in the government?
   Ⓐ They can be senators.
   Ⓑ They can write letters.
   Ⓒ They can elect senators and representatives.
   Ⓓ They can vote.

5. The number of representatives depends upon the _____ of a state.
   Ⓐ senators
   Ⓑ location
   Ⓒ size
   Ⓓ population

Bonus: On the back of this page, explain why it is important for people to vote for their senators and representatives.

©2003 by Evan-Moor Corp. • Nonfiction Reading Practice, Grade 4 • EMC 3315   **The United States Congress**   **21**

Lewis and Clark

Introducing the Topic

1. Reproduce page 23 for individual students, or make a transparency to use with a group or the whole class.

2. Tell students that in 1803 the United States was growing. President Jefferson was interested in obtaining new lands west of the Mississippi River. He sent two explorers, Lewis and Clark, to explore the region. Show the exploration trail of Lewis and Clark to students.

Reading the Selections

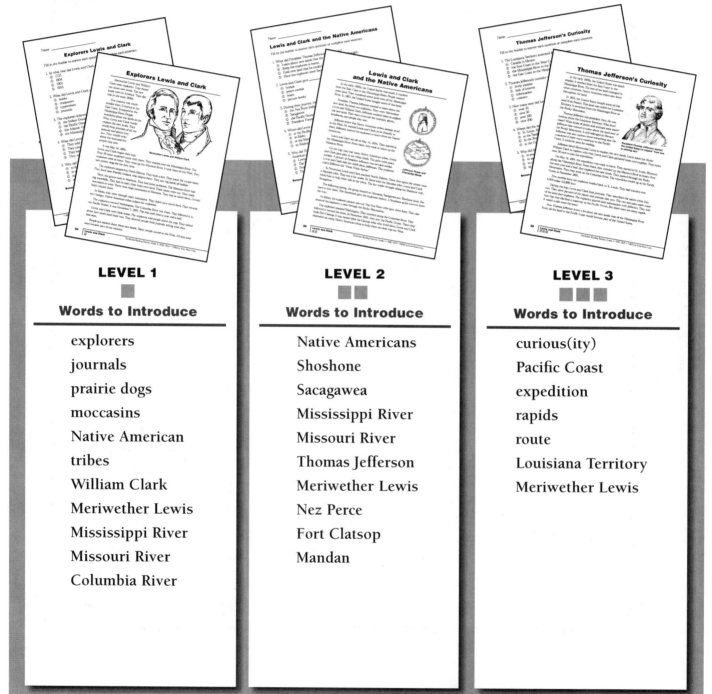

LEVEL 1

Words to Introduce

- explorers
- journals
- prairie dogs
- moccasins
- Native American tribes
- William Clark
- Meriwether Lewis
- Mississippi River
- Missouri River
- Columbia River

LEVEL 2

Words to Introduce

- Native Americans
- Shoshone
- Sacagawea
- Mississippi River
- Missouri River
- Thomas Jefferson
- Meriwether Lewis
- Nez Perce
- Fort Clatsop
- Mandan

LEVEL 3

Words to Introduce

- curious(ity)
- Pacific Coast
- expedition
- rapids
- route
- Louisiana Territory
- Meriwether Lewis

Nonfiction Reading Practice, Grade 4 • EMC 3315 • ©2003 by Evan-Moor Corp.

Lewis and Clark

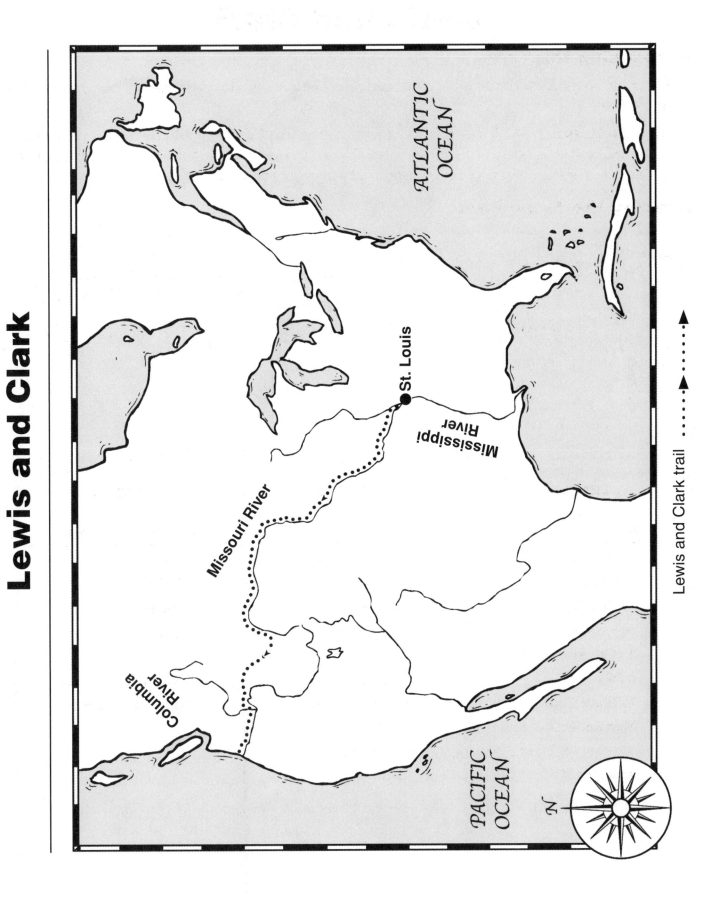

Lewis and Clark trail ·····▶

ATLANTIC OCEAN

PACIFIC OCEAN

St. Louis

Mississippi River

Missouri River

Columbia River

N

Explorers Lewis and Clark

Meriwether Lewis and William Clark were explorers. They found out about new lands. The new lands were in America. They did this in the early 1800s.

Our country was much smaller then. It started at the East Coast. It stopped at the Mississippi River. People wondered about the lands in the West. Lewis and Clark would explore the new lands. They would keep journals of all the animals and plants they saw. They would write about the land and the people they saw.

Meriwether Lewis and William Clark

It was May 14, 1804. Lewis and Clark began their trip. Over 30 other explorers came with them. They started near the Mississippi River. The explorers were in boats. They went up the Missouri River. It took them to the West. They saw prairie dogs for the first time.

The explorers stopped in North Dakota. They built a fort. They spent the winter there. They lived near friendly Indians who helped them. They saw big herds of buffalo.

Next, the group went to Montana. They had some problems. The Missouri River had big waterfalls. They had to carry their boats over land. Their shoes wore out. They made moccasins to wear. There were huge mountains in Montana. They had to climb them. Grizzly bears chased them.

In Idaho, they went through more mountains. They didn't have much food. They became very hungry. Native American tribes helped the explorers.

The explorers reached Washington. The Columbia River was there. They followed it to the Pacific Ocean. It was November 7, 1805. The trip took them a year and a half.

Lewis and Clark went back home. The explorers told people about the trip. They talked about how much land there was. They showed people their journals telling what they had seen.

People got excited about these new lands. Many people moved to the West. All this land soon became part of our country.

Name _____

Explorers Lewis and Clark

Fill in the bubble to answer each question or complete each sentence.

1. In what year did Lewis and Clark start exploring?
   - Ⓐ 1733
   - Ⓑ 1804
   - Ⓒ 1905
   - Ⓓ 1955

2. What did Lewis and Clark use to record what they saw along the trail?
   - Ⓐ books
   - Ⓑ computers
   - Ⓒ typewriters
   - Ⓓ journals

3. The explorers followed the Columbia River to _____.
   - Ⓐ the Indian Ocean
   - Ⓑ the Pacific Ocean
   - Ⓒ the Atlantic Ocean
   - Ⓓ the Mississippi River

4. What did Lewis and Clark do when they went home?
   - Ⓐ They told people about the trip.
   - Ⓑ They saw prairie dogs.
   - Ⓒ They kept the trip a secret.
   - Ⓓ They went back to North Dakota and lived there.

5. Why did Lewis and Clark explore?
   - Ⓐ to find a group of lost people
   - Ⓑ to ride in boats up the Missouri River
   - Ⓒ to find out about new lands
   - Ⓓ to build a fort

Bonus: On the back of this page, draw pictures and label two things Lewis and Clark saw or did on their trip.

Lewis and Clark and the Native Americans

In the early 1800s, the United States was small. It reached from the East Coast to the Mississippi River. People wanted more land. They wondered about land west of the Mississippi River. In 1803, the United States bought some of this land.

President Thomas Jefferson wanted to learn about the new land. He hired two explorers. They were Meriwether Lewis and William Clark. Jefferson wanted them to explore the new land. They were to record the animals, plants, landforms, and people they saw.

Jefferson knew that Native American tribes already lived in the West. He wanted Lewis and Clark to be friendly to them. Jefferson wanted the explorers to learn from the Native Americans.

Lewis and Clark set off on May 14, 1804. They started at the Mississippi River. From there, they rode in boats up the Missouri River.

Jefferson Peace and Friendship Medal

On the trip, they met many Native American tribes. Lewis and Clark gave gifts to the tribal chiefs. The gifts were peace medals. A picture of President Jefferson was on each medal. Lewis and Clark told the chiefs about Jefferson. The explorers called Jefferson the "Great White Father."

In November, Lewis and Clark reached North Dakota. There they spent the winter near a Mandan tribe. They met a fur trader. He lived with the Mandan tribe. Lewis and Clark hired him to help them talk to the tribes. The fur trader brought along his Shoshone wife, Sacagawea.

The following spring, the group headed to Montana. Sacagawea saw Shoshone land. She used to live there. The Shoshones gave the explorers horses. A Shoshone guide showed them the way.

In Idaho, the explorers almost starved. The Nez Perce tribe gave them food. They also showed the explorers a path through the Rocky Mountains.

The explorers reached Washington. They traveled along the Columbia River. They followed it toward the coast. In November 1805, they saw the Pacific Ocean. There they built Fort Clatsop. It was named after the Clatsop tribe who lived there. Lewis and Clark depended on many Native American tribes to help them on their trip out West.

Nonfiction Reading Practice, Grade 4 • EMC 3315 • ©2003 by Evan-Moor Corp.

Name _____

Lewis and Clark and the Native Americans

Fill in the bubble to answer each question or complete each sentence.

1. What did President Thomas Jefferson want to do?
   Ⓐ Learn about new lands that the United States just bought.
   Ⓑ Keep the explorers at home.
   Ⓒ Find new land that he could live on while he was president.
   Ⓓ Have the explorers meet Sacagawea and bring her back.

2. Lewis and Clark gave _____ to the tribal chiefs.
   Ⓐ horses
   Ⓑ peace medals
   Ⓒ boats
   Ⓓ picture books

3. During their journey, the explorers told the chiefs about _____.
   Ⓐ the Nez Perce Indians
   Ⓑ Sacagawea
   Ⓒ the Pacific Ocean
   Ⓓ President Thomas Jefferson

4. Where did Lewis and Clark start their journey?
   Ⓐ at the Pacific Ocean
   Ⓑ in Idaho
   Ⓒ at the Mississippi River
   Ⓓ in Washington

5. Why did Thomas Jefferson want Lewis and Clark to be friendly to the Native American tribes?
   Ⓐ Lewis and Clark could get medals from the Indians.
   Ⓑ The Native Americans would help build Fort Clatsop.
   Ⓒ President Jefferson knew the Native American chiefs.
   Ⓓ The Native Americans lived on the lands they would be exploring.

Bonus: On the back of this page, explain two ways the Native Americans helped Lewis and Clark.

Thomas Jefferson's Curiosity

In the early 1800s, the United States was much smaller. It reached from the East Coast to the Mississippi River. The rest of the land belonged to other countries. Native American tribes also lived throughout the land.

In 1803, the United States bought some of this land from France. This land was called the Louisiana Territory. It stretched from the Mississippi River to the Rocky Mountains.

President Thomas Jefferson wanted the United States to expand "from sea to shining sea."

Thomas Jefferson was president then. He was curious about the Louisiana Territory. Who lived there? What kinds of plants and animals were there? Jefferson also wanted to know about the land west of the Rocky Mountains. It still belonged to Mexico. Jefferson was also curious about something else. He wondered if there was a waterway to the Pacific Coast. It could be used for trading.

Jefferson hired Meriwether Lewis to explore the new lands. Lewis asked his friend William Clark to explore with him. Lewis and Clark gathered boats and supplies. They hired over 30 men to join the expedition.

On May 14, 1804, the expedition was ready to leave. They started in St. Louis, Missouri, along the Mississippi River. From there, they traveled up the Missouri River in boats. Over the next year and a half, they explored the new lands. They passed through the Rocky Mountains. Then they went on the Columbia River. The expedition ended up at the Pacific Ocean in November 1805.

Five months later, the explorers headed back to St. Louis. They had traveled over 8,000 miles (12,800 km).

During the trip, Lewis and Clark kept journals. They described the native tribes they met. They drew pictures of the plants and animals they saw. The two men also made maps of the land they explored. The explorers shared their information with Jefferson. They told him that they did find a waterway to the Pacific Ocean. But there were too many rapids. It wasn't a safe route for boats.

Now Thomas Jefferson knew a lot about the new lands west of the Mississippi River. Soon, all the land to the Pacific Coast would become part of the United States.

Nonfiction Reading Practice, Grade 4 • EMC 3315 • ©2003 by Evan-Moor Corp.

Name _____

Thomas Jefferson's Curiosity

Fill in the bubble to answer each question or complete each sentence.

1. The Louisiana Territory stretched from _____.
   Ⓐ Canada to Mexico
   Ⓑ the East Coast to the West Coast
   Ⓒ the Mississippi River to the Rocky Mountains
   Ⓓ the East Coast to the Mississippi River

2. Thomas Jefferson's curiosity was strong. What does the word *curiosity* mean?
   Ⓐ lively interest
   Ⓑ lack of interest
   Ⓒ information
   Ⓓ concern

3. How many men did Lewis and Clark hire to join the expedition?
   Ⓐ over 10
   Ⓑ over 30
   Ⓒ over 100
   Ⓓ over 200

4. Where did the expedition start?
   Ⓐ St. Louis, Missouri
   Ⓑ at the Pacific Coast
   Ⓒ in the Rocky Mountains
   Ⓓ at the Columbia River

5. Why did Jefferson want to know if there was a waterway to the Pacific Ocean?
   Ⓐ to see if Lewis and Clark needed to travel in boats or by foot
   Ⓑ to use it as drinking water for the country
   Ⓒ to use it for trading
   Ⓓ to use it for fishing

Bonus: On the back of this page, explain the three reasons why President Jefferson wanted Lewis and Clark to lead an exploration west.

The Civil War

Introducing the Topic

1. Reproduce page 31 for individual students, or make a transparency to use with a group or the whole class.

2. Show students the map of the United States. Explain that this is what our country looked like in 1861. Eleven southern states had seceded. They believed in the need for slavery. They were called the Confederacy. The 22 northern states were called the Union. These states did not believe slavery should be legal. All this and more led to the Civil War.

Reading the Selections

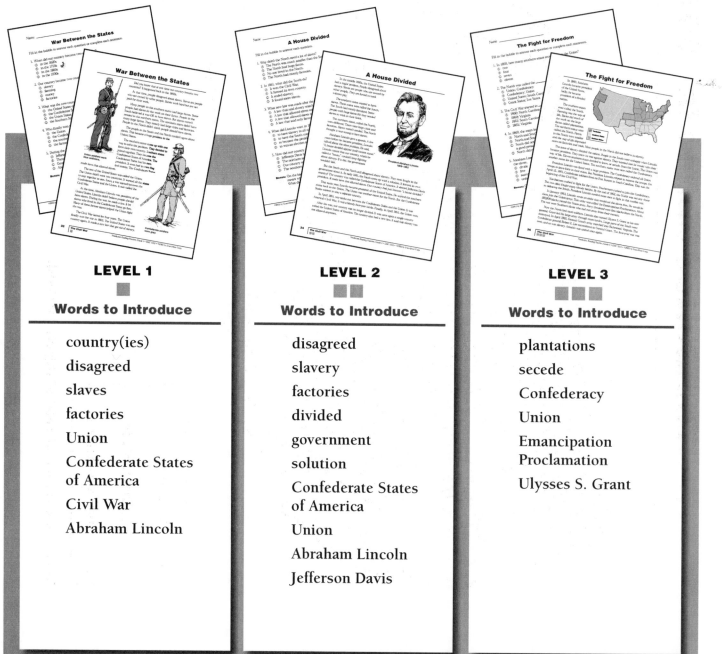

LEVEL 1

Words to Introduce

country(ies)

disagreed

slaves

factories

Union

Confederate States of America

Civil War

Abraham Lincoln

LEVEL 2

Words to Introduce

disagreed

slavery

factories

divided

government

solution

Confederate States of America

Union

Abraham Lincoln

Jefferson Davis

LEVEL 3

Words to Introduce

plantations

secede

Confederacy

Union

Emancipation Proclamation

Ulysses S. Grant

Nonfiction Reading Practice, Grade 4 • EMC 3315 • ©2003 by Evan-Moor Corp.

The United States in 1861 *

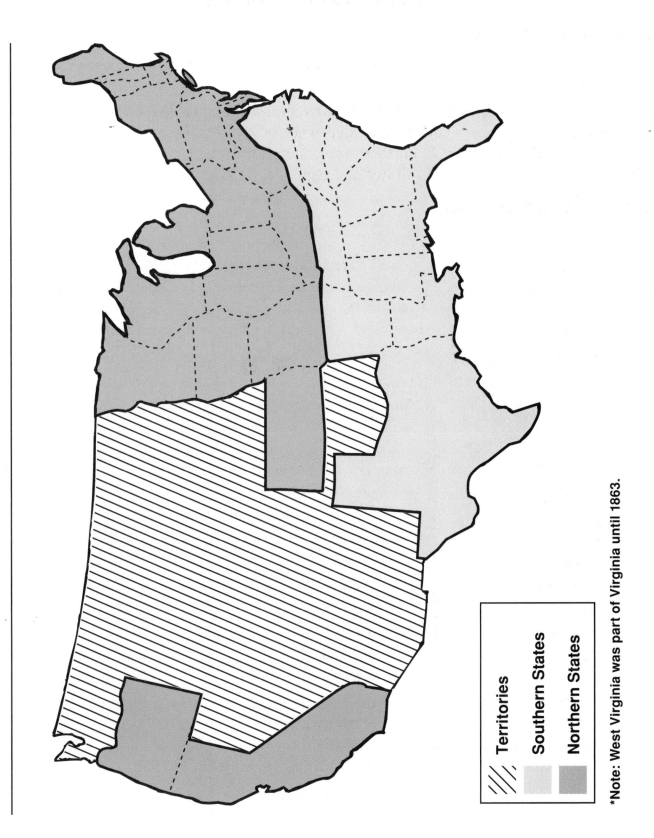

Territories

Southern States

Northern States

*Note: West Virginia was part of Virginia until 1863.

War Between the States

Union soldiers wore blue uniforms.

Did you know that at one time our country became two countries? It happened back in the 1860s.

At that time, people disagreed about slaves. Slaves are people who are owned by other people. Slaves work hard but are not paid for their work.

Many people in the southern states had large farms. Some people had slaves do the work on their farms. People in the South believed it was OK to have slaves. But slaves weren't needed in the northern states. The northern states didn't have many large farms. They mostly had large cities and factories. People in the North didn't think people should have slaves.

The people in the South and the North couldn't agree about slaves. This became a huge problem in the United States.

The southern states came up with one way to solve the problem. They decided to form their own country. Southern states joined together. They became the Confederate States of America. The Confederate States had its own president. It even had its own flag and money. The Confederate States made laws that allowed slaves.

The rest of the United States was called the Union. The Union didn't want two countries. It wanted all the states to stay together as one. Soon, a war started between the Confederate States and the Union. It was called the Civil War.

At the time, Abraham Lincoln was president of the United States. Lincoln didn't believe people should have slaves. During the war, he made a law. It let slaves who lived in the Confederate States go free. Many of these former slaves helped the Union fight the war.

The Civil War lasted for four years. The Union finally won the war in 1865. The United States was one country again. It made a new law that got rid of slavery.

Confederate soldiers wore gray.

Nonfiction Reading Practice, Grade 4 • EMC 3315 • ©2003 by Evan-Moor Corp.

Name _____

War Between the States

Fill in the bubble to answer each question or complete each sentence.

1. When did our country become two countries?
   - Ⓐ in the 1620s
   - Ⓑ in the 1750s
   - Ⓒ in the 1860s
   - Ⓓ in the 1930s

2. Our country became two countries when people disagreed about _____.
   - Ⓐ slavery
   - Ⓑ farming
   - Ⓒ money
   - Ⓓ factories

3. What was the new country called in the South?
   - Ⓐ the United States of America
   - Ⓑ the Confederate States of America
   - Ⓒ the Union States of America
   - Ⓓ the Southern States of America

4. Who finally won the Civil War?
   - Ⓐ the Union
   - Ⓑ the Confederate States of America
   - Ⓒ the southern states
   - Ⓓ the farmers

5. During the Civil War, who was president of the United States?
   - Ⓐ Jefferson Davis
   - Ⓑ Thomas Jefferson
   - Ⓒ George Washington
   - Ⓓ Abraham Lincoln

Bonus: On the back of this page, explain why the South had slaves.

A House Divided

In the middle 1800s, the United States had a major problem. People disagreed about slavery. Slaves are people who are owned by other people. They are forced to work without pay.

The southern states wanted to have slaves. These states were called the South. The South had mostly farmland. Some people with huge farms felt they needed slaves to work in their fields.

The northern states, called the North, were different. There were large cities and factories. Slaves weren't needed. The North thought it was wrong to have slaves.

Abraham Lincoln gave a speech. A few years before he became president, Lincoln talked about the slave problem. He said, "A house divided against itself cannot stand." Lincoln meant that our country, which he called a "house," couldn't keep fighting about slavery. If it did, the government wouldn't last.

President Abraham Lincoln
1809–1865

But the South and the North still disagreed about slavery. They even fought in the government about it. In early 1861, the South came up with a solution. It formed its own country! The country was called the Confederate States of America. It elected Jefferson Davis president. It made laws that allowed slaves. Our country had just become "a house divided."

That same year, Lincoln became president of the United States. He wanted the southern states back in the Union. The Union was another name for the North. But the Confederate States wanted to stay a separate country.

In April 1861, war broke out between the Confederate States and the Union. It was America's Civil War. It was a bloody four-year battle. Finally, in April 1865, the Union won.

After the war, our country was no longer divided. It was once again a single country called the United States of America. The country also had a new law. It said that slavery was not allowed anymore.

Nonfiction Reading Practice, Grade 4 • EMC 3315 • ©2003 by Evan-Moor Corp.

Name _____

A House Divided

Fill in the bubble to answer each question.

1. Why didn't the North need a lot of slaves?
   - Ⓐ The North was much smaller than the South.
   - Ⓑ The North had huge farms.
   - Ⓒ No one lived in the North.
   - Ⓓ The North had mostly factories.

2. In 1861, what did the South do?
   - Ⓐ It won the Civil War.
   - Ⓑ It formed its own country.
   - Ⓒ It ended slavery.
   - Ⓓ It found more slaves.

3. What new law was made after the Civil War?
   - Ⓐ A law that said slavery wasn't allowed in the North or the South.
   - Ⓑ A law that allowed slaves only in the South.
   - Ⓒ A law that allowed slaves only in the North.
   - Ⓓ A law that said only farmers could have slaves.

4. What did Lincoln want in 1861?
   - Ⓐ to have slavery in all states
   - Ⓑ to have the South come back into the Union
   - Ⓒ to become the president of the Confederate States
   - Ⓓ to win an election against Jefferson Davis

5. How did our country become "a house divided"?
   - Ⓐ Jefferson Davis became the president.
   - Ⓑ The northern states started having slaves.
   - Ⓒ Our country was divided up into many states.
   - Ⓓ The southern states became their own country.

Bonus: On the back of this page, explain in your own words what Lincoln meant when he said, "A house divided against itself cannot stand." What did he mean by a "house"?

The Fight for Freedom

In 1860, Abraham Lincoln became president of the United States. Sadly, he became president of a divided nation.

The southern states were called the South. Farming was the way of life. Slaves did much of the work on the large farms called plantations. The northern states were called the North. Farms in the North were smaller, and the way of life depended more on factories and trade. Most people in the North did not believe in slavery.

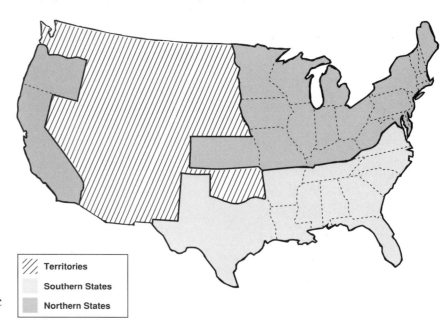

Territories
Southern States
Northern States

The issue of slavery divided the nation. People in the South were unhappy when Lincoln became president. They knew he was against slavery. They worried that he would ruin their way of life. Eleven southern states decided to leave, or secede, from the Union. The Union was another name for the United States. The southern states were now called the Confederacy.

President Lincoln was faced with a huge problem. The Confederacy ordered all Union troops to leave forts in their states. But President Lincoln refused to remove the troops. On April 12, 1861, Confederate soldiers fired on Fort Sumter in South Carolina. This was the beginning of the Civil War.

Northerners rushed to fight for the Union. Southerners rushed to join the Confederacy. The two sides fought many bloody battles. By the end of 1862, the North was not any closer to defeating the South. President Lincoln needed more men to fight in this terrible war.

In January 1863, Lincoln wrote an order that would set the slaves free. He would let them join the Union army. This order was called the Emancipation Proclamation. About 180,000 blacks joined the Union army. Forty thousand were free blacks from the North. The rest were Southern slaves who had run away from their owners.

Now the North had more soldiers. Lincoln also named Ulysses S. Grant as his new general. Grant led his large army through more battles. Large parts of the South were destroyed. In April 1865, General Grant's army marched into Richmond, Virginia. The Confederate general Robert E. Lee surrendered to General Grant. The four-year war was over, and so was slavery. America was united once again.

Nonfiction Reading Practice, Grade 4 • EMC 3315 • ©2003 by Evan-Moor Corp.

Name _____

The Fight for Freedom

Fill in the bubble to answer each question or complete each statement.

1. In 1860, how many southern states seceded from the Union?
   - Ⓐ two
   - Ⓑ four
   - Ⓒ seven
   - Ⓓ eleven

2. The North was called the _____ and the South was called the _____.
   - Ⓐ Union; Confederacy
   - Ⓑ Confederacy; Union
   - Ⓒ United States; South Carolina
   - Ⓓ Grant States; Lee States

3. The Civil War started in _____ in _____.
   - Ⓐ 1860; North Carolina
   - Ⓑ 1860; Virginia
   - Ⓒ 1861; South Carolina
   - Ⓓ 1865; Virginia

4. In 1860, the main issue that divided the nation was that the _____.
   - Ⓐ North and South could not agree on farming practices
   - Ⓑ North and South did not trade with each other
   - Ⓒ South did not like Abraham Lincoln, but the North thought he was a good president
   - Ⓓ North did not believe in slavery, but the South thought it was necessary

5. Abraham Lincoln signed a proclamation to emancipate, or to _____, the slaves.
   - Ⓐ divide
   - Ⓑ free
   - Ⓒ surrender
   - Ⓓ unite

Bonus: On the back of this page, write how the Civil War changed the United States.

Floating Continents

Introducing the Topic

1. Reproduce page 39 for individual students, or make a transparency to use with a group or the whole class.

2. Show students the maps. Have them compare Earth 250 million years ago, 180 million years ago, and present-day. Have them name the continents (Africa, Antarctica, Asia, Australia, Europe, North America, and South America). Have them name the oceans (Arctic, Atlantic, Indian, and Pacific).

Reading the Selections

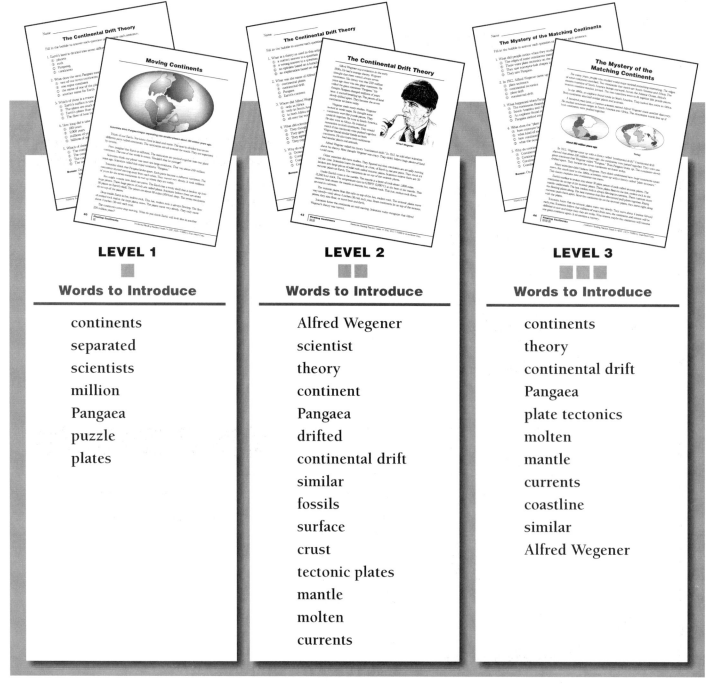

LEVEL 1

Words to Introduce

continents

separated

scientists

million

Pangaea

puzzle

plates

LEVEL 2

Words to Introduce

Alfred Wegener

scientist

theory

continent

Pangaea

drifted

continental drift

similar

fossils

surface

crust

tectonic plates

mantle

molten

currents

LEVEL 3

Words to Introduce

continents

theory

continental drift

Pangaea

plate tectonics

molten

mantle

currents

coastline

similar

Alfred Wegener

Nonfiction Reading Practice, Grade 4 • EMC 3315 • ©2003 by Evan-Moor Corp.

Maps of Earth

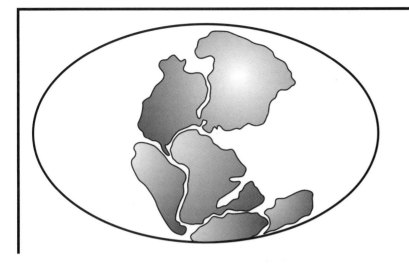

250 Million Years Ago

Earth as it looked 250 million years ago.

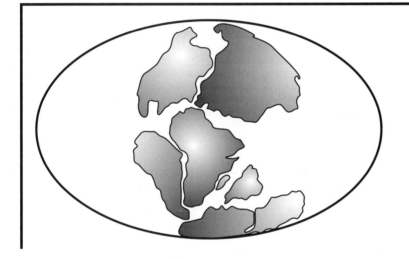

180 Million Years Ago

Pangaea began to separate into smaller pieces 180 million years ago.

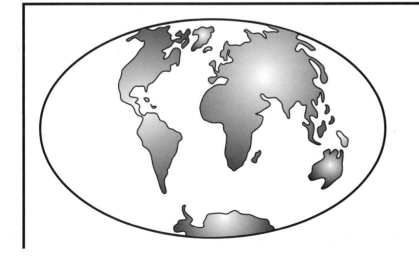

Today

Earth as it appears today. How many continents do you see? How many oceans do you see?

Moving Continents

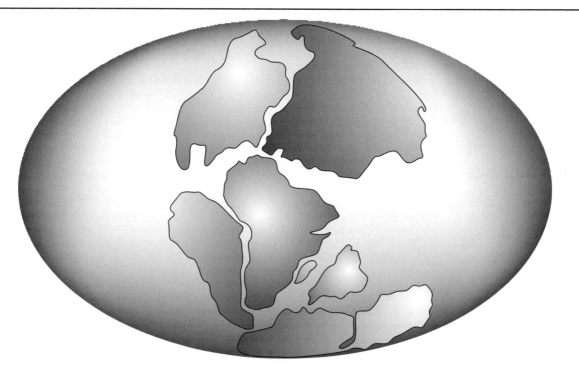

Scientists think Pangaea began separating into smaller pieces about 180 million years ago.

Think of our Earth. You know there is land and water. The land is divided into seven different parts called continents. The continents are all around the world. They are separated by oceans.

Now imagine that Earth is different. The continents are pushed together into one giant continent. The rest of the world is ocean. Wouldn't that be strange?

Scientists think our planet was once one large continent. That was about 250 million years ago. Scientists called this super continent "Pangaea."

Scientists think that Pangaea broke apart. Each piece became a different continent. The continents started moving away from each other. They moved very slowly. It took millions of years for the seven continents to end up where they are today.

You might wonder how land can move. The Earth has a rocky shell that is broken up into large pieces. These huge pieces of rock are called plates. Scientists believe there are about 30 plates on Earth's shell. The plates are about 60 miles (100 km) deep. The seven continents sit on top of the plates.

Deep inside Earth is hot, molten rock. This hot, molten rock is always flowing. The flow of melted rock makes the large plates move. The plates move very slowly. They only move about 4 inches (10 cm) each year.

The continents never stop moving. What do you think Earth will look like in another 250 million years?

 Nonfiction Reading Practice, Grade 4 • EMC 3315 • ©2003 by Evan-Moor Corp.

Name _____

Moving Continents

Fill in the bubble to answer each question or complete each sentence.

1. Earth's land is divided into seven different parts called _____.
   - Ⓐ planets
   - Ⓑ rock
   - Ⓒ Pangaeag
   - Ⓓ continents

2. What does the term *Pangaea* mean?
   - Ⓐ one of our seven continents
   - Ⓑ one super continent
   - Ⓒ the name of one of the plates
   - Ⓓ another name for Earth

3. Which of these is a reason land can move?
   - Ⓐ Earth's surface is one solid piece.
   - Ⓑ The plates are stuck to the Earth.
   - Ⓒ Earth's plates float on melted rock.
   - Ⓓ The flow of heat inside the Earth melts the plates.

4. How long did it take for Earth's plates to move to where they are today?
   - Ⓐ 100 years
   - Ⓑ 5,000 years
   - Ⓒ millions of years
   - Ⓓ billions of years

5. Which of these statements is known to be true?
   - Ⓐ The continents never stop moving.
   - Ⓑ The continents have stopped moving.
   - Ⓒ The continents will stop moving in one million years.
   - Ⓓ The seven continents will become one continent again.

Bonus: On the back of this page, draw a picture of what you think Earth will look like in another 250 million years. Write two sentences to describe what you drew.

The Continental Drift Theory

Alfred Wegener was a scientist in the early 1900s. He had a strange theory. Wegener thought that there weren't always seven continents. His theory was that 250 million years ago there was one giant continent. He called the giant continent "Pangaea." He thought Pangaea changed millions of years later. It started breaking up. The pieces of land slowly drifted apart. They became the seven continents we know today.

Alfred Wegener

Wegener made many studies. Wegener looked at world maps. He thought some continents were like puzzle pieces. They could fit together. He went to South America. He also went to Africa. He looked at mountains on both continents. They would match if the continents were pushed together. Wegener found similar fossils on both continents. He also knew both continents had similar plants and animals.

Alfred Wegener called his theory "continental drift." In 1912, he told other scientists about his theory. Most thought Wegener was crazy. They didn't believe huge pieces of land could move.

Other scientists did more studies. They figured out that continents are actually moving all the time. Scientists know the surface, or crust, of Earth is not one piece. They think it's broken into large pieces of solid rock called tectonic plates. Scientists believe there are 30 tectonic plates on Earth. The continents lie on top of the tectonic plates.

Under Earth's crust is the mantle. The mantle is a layer of rock about 1,800 miles (2,900 km) thick. The temperature rises to 6,700°F (3,700°C) at the base of the mantle. This extreme heat causes the mantle to become hot, molten rock. This hot, molten rock flows around in currents.

The tectonic plates float like rafts on top of the hot, molten rock. The tectonic plates move very slowly—only about 4 inches (10 cm) each year. Since continents lie on top of the tectonic plates, they also float, or move back and forth.

Scientists know the continents are still moving. Scientists today recognize that Alfred Wegener's theory was correct.

Nonfiction Reading Practice, Grade 4 • EMC 3315 • ©2003 by Evan-Moor Corp.

Name _____

The Continental Drift Theory

Fill in the bubble to answer each question.

1. What is a *theory* as used in this article?
   - Ⓐ a correct answer to a question
   - Ⓑ a wrong answer to a question
   - Ⓒ an opinion based on a hunch or feeling
   - Ⓓ an explanation based on observation and reasoning

2. What was the name of Alfred Wegener's theory?
   - Ⓐ continental plates
   - Ⓑ continental drift
   - Ⓒ Pangaea
   - Ⓓ Earth's currents

3. Where did Alfred Wegener find clues to prove his theory?
   - Ⓐ only in Africa
   - Ⓑ only in South America
   - Ⓒ in both Africa and South America
   - Ⓓ all over the world

4. What did scientists in the early 1900s think about Wegener's theory?
   - Ⓐ They thought it was crazy.
   - Ⓑ They gave him many awards for it.
   - Ⓒ They agreed with him.
   - Ⓓ They copied his idea right away.

5. Why do scientists think continents can move?
   - Ⓐ Ocean currents cause the continents to move.
   - Ⓑ Continents lie on top of tectonic plates that float on hot, molten rock.
   - Ⓒ Continents lie below tectonic plates that move.
   - Ⓓ Continents are huge pieces of land.

Bonus: Pretend you are Alfred Wegener. On the back of this page, explain your theory.

The Mystery of the Matching Continents

For many years, people who studied world maps noticed something interesting. The edges of some continents matched. Two continents that match are South America and Africa. The eastern coastline of South America bumps outward. Across the Atlantic Ocean, Africa's western coastline notches inward. The two coastlines seem to fit together like puzzle pieces.

In the 1800s, an explorer found rocks in South America. They looked like rocks in Africa. Both continents also had similar plants and animals.

A hundred years later, a German scientist named Alfred Wegener made another discovery. He studied mountain ranges in South America and Africa. The mountains would line up if both continents were pushed together.

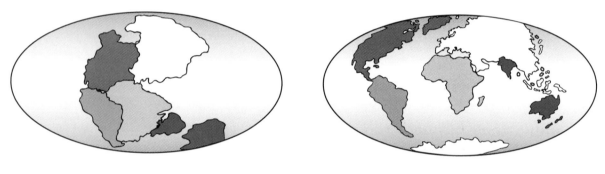

About 250 million years ago   **Today**

In 1912, Wegener came up with a theory called "continental drift." Continental drift showed that about 250 million years ago, the continents were joined together. They were one giant continent that Wegener called "Pangaea." Then Pangaea broke up. The continents slowly drifted apart. They became the seven continents we know today.

Many scientists didn't believe Wegener. They didn't understand how huge continents could move. But much later in the 1960s, scientists came up with a theory called "plate tectonics." This theory explains how continents can move.

Earth's surface is broken into about 30 giant pieces of rock called tectonic plates. The continents lie on top of the tectonic plates. These plates float on the hot, molten rock in the mantle underneath. The hot, molten rock is always flowing in currents. These currents move the floating plates along. The heat currents that flow downward pull plates together. Rising currents push them apart. Since the continents lie on the tectonic plates, they move right along with the plates.

Scientists know that the tectonic plates move very slowly. They move about 4 inches (10 cm) each year. Scientists believe that millions of years from now, the continents and oceans will be different in size and shape than they are today. Who knows, maybe the continents will become one giant continent again. It all remains a mystery.

Name _____

The Mystery of the Matching Continents

Fill in the bubble to answer each question or complete each sentence.

1. What did people notice when they studied world maps?
   - Ⓐ The edges of some continents matched like puzzle pieces.
   - Ⓑ There were plate tectonics on the map.
   - Ⓒ They saw conveyor-belt shapes in the oceans.
   - Ⓓ They saw Pangaea.

2. In 1912, Alfred Wegener came up with a theory called _____.
   - Ⓐ plate tectonics
   - Ⓑ continental tectonics
   - Ⓒ plate drift
   - Ⓓ continental drift

3. What happened when Pangaea broke up?
   - Ⓐ The continents floated apart.
   - Ⓑ South America and Africa joined together.
   - Ⓒ An explorer found rocks in South America.
   - Ⓓ Pangaea melted into Earth.

4. What does the "plate tectonics" theory explain?
   - Ⓐ how conveyor belts work on Earth
   - Ⓑ what kind of rocks were in South America
   - Ⓒ how continents can move
   - Ⓓ what the ocean floor looks like

5. Why do continents move?
   - Ⓐ Continents lie beneath the moving tectonic plates.
   - Ⓑ Continents lie on tectonic plates that float on hot, molten rock.
   - Ⓒ Continents float on oceans.
   - Ⓓ Continents float on conveyor belts.

Bonus: On the back of this page, explain the theory of plate tectonics.

Electric Light

Introducing the Topic

1. Reproduce page 47 for individual students, or make a transparency to use with a group or the whole class.

2. First, ask students to imagine a light bulb. Have them describe the different parts that make up a light bulb. Show students the illustration of the light bulb. Tell students they will be reading about how electricity makes a light bulb glow.

Reading the Selections

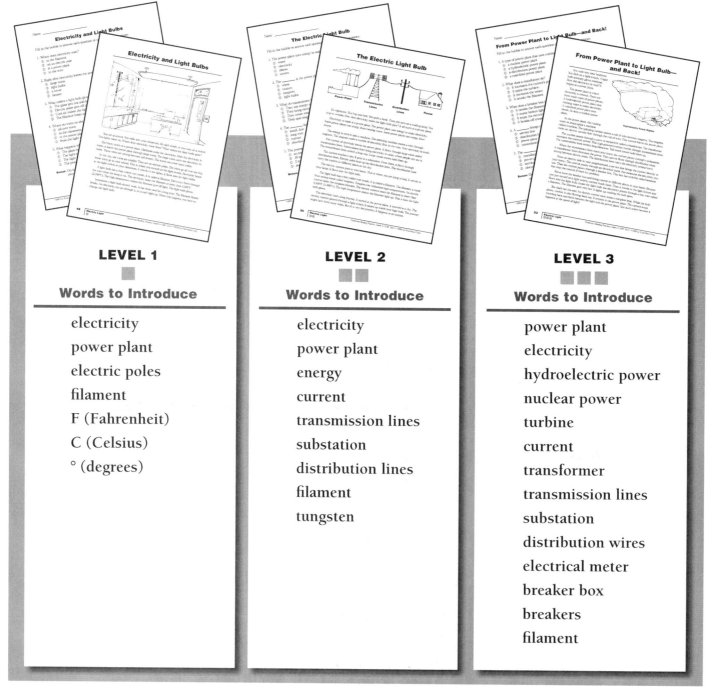

LEVEL 1

Words to Introduce

electricity

power plant

electric poles

filament

F (Fahrenheit)

C (Celsius)

° (degrees)

LEVEL 2

Words to Introduce

electricity

power plant

energy

current

transmission lines

substation

distribution lines

filament

tungsten

LEVEL 3

Words to Introduce

power plant

electricity

hydroelectric power

nuclear power

turbine

current

transformer

transmission lines

substation

distribution wires

electrical meter

breaker box

breakers

filament

Diagram of a Light Bulb

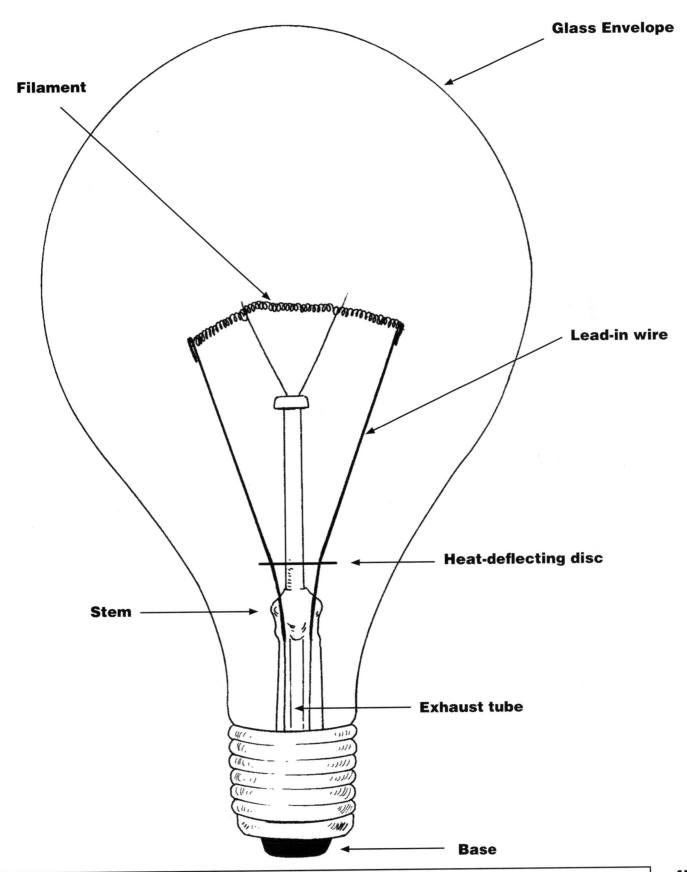

Glass Envelope

Filament

Lead-in wire

Heat-deflecting disc

Stem

Exhaust tube

Base

Electricity and Light Bulbs

You are at school. You walk into your classroom. It's dark inside, so you turn on a switch. The lights come on. Where does electricity come from? What makes the light bulbs glow?

Electricity starts at a power plant. Machines make the electricity. After the electricity is made, it leaves the power plant through large wires. The large wires carry the electricity to cities. These wires are strung between tall towers. The wires can cover many miles.

In the city, the wires are smaller. They are on electric poles. The wires go all over the city. Some wires go to your school. This is where you turned on the light switch. Electricity heads to the light switch in your classroom. It travels to the lights. It flows into the light bulbs.

A light bulb has a thin coiled wire inside. It is called a filament. Electricity flows through the wire when the lamp is on. The electricity heats the filament to more than 4,500°F (2,500°C). The high temperature makes the filament give off light. The light bulb glows.

Sometimes a light bulb doesn't work. It has been used for a long time. The filament finally breaks. No electricity can go through it, so it can't light up. When this happens, you have to change the light bulb.

Nonfiction Reading Practice, Grade 4 • EMC 3315 • ©2003 by Evan-Moor Corp.

Name _____

Electricity and Light Bulbs

Fill in the bubble to answer each question or complete each sentence.

1. Where does electricity start?
   - Ⓐ in the filament
   - Ⓑ on an electric pole
   - Ⓒ at a power plant
   - Ⓓ in the wire

2. Right after electricity leaves the power plant, it travels through _____.
   - Ⓐ large wires
   - Ⓑ light bulbs
   - Ⓒ a tower
   - Ⓓ houses

3. What makes a light bulb glow?
   - Ⓐ The glass gets hot and lights up.
   - Ⓑ Electric poles give off electricity.
   - Ⓒ Cool air makes the light bulb snap on.
   - Ⓓ The filament heats up.

4. Where do wires on electric poles go next?
   - Ⓐ all over town
   - Ⓑ in the classroom
   - Ⓒ to the power plant
   - Ⓓ from the light switch to the light bulb

5. What happens when the filament breaks?
   - Ⓐ The glass bulb also breaks.
   - Ⓑ The light switch gets hot.
   - Ⓒ The light bulb doesn't glow.
   - Ⓓ The power plant can't make electricity.

Bonus: On the back of this page, explain what happens to the filament when electricity flows through it.

The Electric Light Bulb

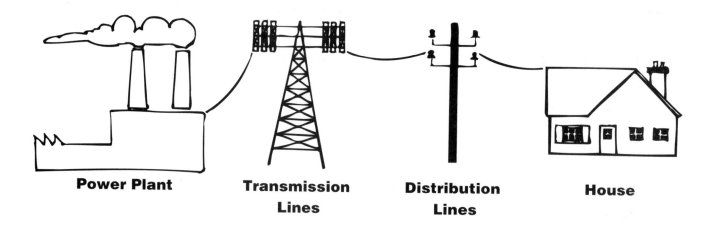

Power Plant   **Transmission**   **Distribution**   **House**
                              Lines   **Lines**

It's nighttime. You hop into bed. You grab a book. Then you turn on a reading lamp. You stop to wonder. How does electricity make the light bulb glow? It all starts at a power plant.

Electricity is made at a power plant. The power plant uses energy to make electricity. Some power plants use energy from moving water. Some power plants use energy from steam.

The energy is used to spin a machine. The spinning machine moves a wire through magnets. The magnets make a current of electricity flow in the wire. Now electricity is made.

The current of electricity leaves the power plant. It flows through large wires called transmission lines. Transmission lines bring electricity to cities, where people can use it. The transmission lines stretch a long way. Large metal towers hold them up.

The current reaches a city. It goes to a substation. From there, it flows through distribution lines. Electric poles hold up the distribution lines. The distribution lines carry the current to different places in the city.

The electric current goes to your home. This is where you are lying in bed. It travels to your lamp. It flows into the light bulb.

The light bulb has a thin coiled wire inside. It is called a filament. The filament is made from strong metal called tungsten. Tungsten can withstand high temperatures. An electric current heats the tungsten filament. The electric current heats the filament to more than 4,500°F (2,500°C). The high temperature makes the filament light up. This is how the light bulb glows.

The electricity had a long journey. It started at the power plant. It traveled to a city. The electric current passed through a light switch. It ended up inside your light bulb. The journey might have been many miles. But it's a very fast journey. It happens in an instant.

   Nonfiction Reading Practice, Grade 4 • EMC 3315 • ©2003 by Evan-Moor Corp.

Name _____

The Electric Light Bulb

Fill in the bubble to answer each question or complete each sentence.

1. The power plant uses energy to make _____.
   - Ⓐ water
   - Ⓑ electricity
   - Ⓒ plants
   - Ⓓ towers

2. The _____ at the power plant make a current of electricity flow.
   - Ⓐ wires
   - Ⓑ heaters
   - Ⓒ magnets
   - Ⓓ light bulbs

3. What do transmission lines do?
   - Ⓐ They use energy to make electricity.
   - Ⓑ They bring electricity to cities, where people can use it.
   - Ⓒ They create steam for the power plant.
   - Ⓓ They spin magnets at the power plant.

4. The _____ lines carry the current to different places in the city.
   - Ⓐ small, fine
   - Ⓑ long wire
   - Ⓒ current
   - Ⓓ distribution

5. The journey from the power plant to a home happens in _____.
   - Ⓐ an instant
   - Ⓑ 30 seconds
   - Ⓒ 2 to 3 minutes
   - Ⓓ about 10 minutes

Bonus: On the back of this page, explain why power plants are important.

From Power Plant to Light Bulb— and Back!

You walk into your bedroom. You flick on a light switch. A light bulb instantly glows overhead. How did electricity do that? It begins at a power plant.

The power plant is where electricity is created. There are three main types of power plants. A hydroelectric power plant uses rushing water to make electricity. A coal-fired power plant uses steam. So does a nuclear power plant.

Hydroelectric Power Station

At the power plant, the rushing water or steam spins a machine called a turbine. The spinning turbine moves a coil of wire between magnets. The magnets make an electric current flow through the coil of wire. This current leaves the power plant.

The current passes through a piece of equipment called a transformer. The transformer increases the current's power. This high-powered current travels through transmission lines. The transmission lines stretch long distances. Tall metal towers hold them up.

When the transmission lines reach your town, the current passes through a substation. A transformer there decreases the power. This current flows through distribution wires strung between electric poles. The distribution lines carry the electricity around town.

From an electric pole in your neighborhood, a service line brings the current directly to your home. The current passes through an electrical meter that measures the electricity you use. Then the current passes through a breaker box. This box has switches called breakers that stop the current if there is a problem.

Wires leave the breaker box and bring current to different places in your home. Because you just turned on a light switch, current heads there. Then it travels to the light fixture and flows into the light bulb. Inside the light bulb, the electricity passes through a tiny wire called a filament. The filament gets very hot. It lights up, making the bulb glow.

But that's not the end. An electric current must make a complete loop. While the bulb glows, current is also flowing back out. It returns to the power plant. The current keeps traveling back and forth between the light and the power plant. You don't notice because it happens at the speed of light!

Nonfiction Reading Practice, Grade 4 • EMC 3315 • ©2003 by Evan-Moor Corp.

From Power Plant to Light Bulb—and Back!

Fill in the bubble to answer each question or complete each sentence.

1. A type of power plant that uses rushing water to make electricity is _____.
   - Ⓐ a nuclear power plant
   - Ⓑ a hydroelectric power plant
   - Ⓒ a distribution power plant
   - Ⓓ a coal-fired power plant

2. What does a transformer do?
   - Ⓐ It increases the current's power.
   - Ⓑ It spins the turbine.
   - Ⓒ It increases the steam.
   - Ⓓ It breaks the filament.

3. What does a breaker box do?
   - Ⓐ It breaks the filament in a light bulb.
   - Ⓑ It stores broken light bulbs.
   - Ⓒ It stops the electric current if there's a problem.
   - Ⓓ It breaks off transmission lines.

4. A _____ brings current directly to your house.
   - Ⓐ service line
   - Ⓑ distribution line
   - Ⓒ power plant wire
   - Ⓓ transmission line

5. The _____ must make a complete loop.
   - Ⓐ transformer
   - Ⓑ power plant
   - Ⓒ service line
   - Ⓓ electric current

Bonus: On the back of this page, explain how the three types of power plants make electricity.

Heredity

Introducing the Topic

1. Reproduce page 55 for individual students, or make a transparency to use with a group or the whole class.

2. Show students the picture. Ask if they've ever been to a family reunion—a get-together of many family members, including aunts, uncles, cousins, and grandparents. Ask students what they notice about how the people look in the picture. The students should notice that the family members might have similar traits such as hair color, eye color, and height. Then show students the heredity diagram.

Reading the Selections

LEVEL 1

Words to Introduce

traits

similar

physical features

special

cell

chromosomes

genes

features

exactly

LEVEL 2

Words to Introduce

similar

traits

produce

offspring

body cells

chromosomes

genes

LEVEL 3

Words to Introduce

Gregor Mendel

heredity

traits

experimented

offspring

bred

identical

generation

chromosomes

genes

Nonfiction Reading Practice, Grade 4 • EMC 3315 • ©2003 by Evan-Moor Corp.

Heredity

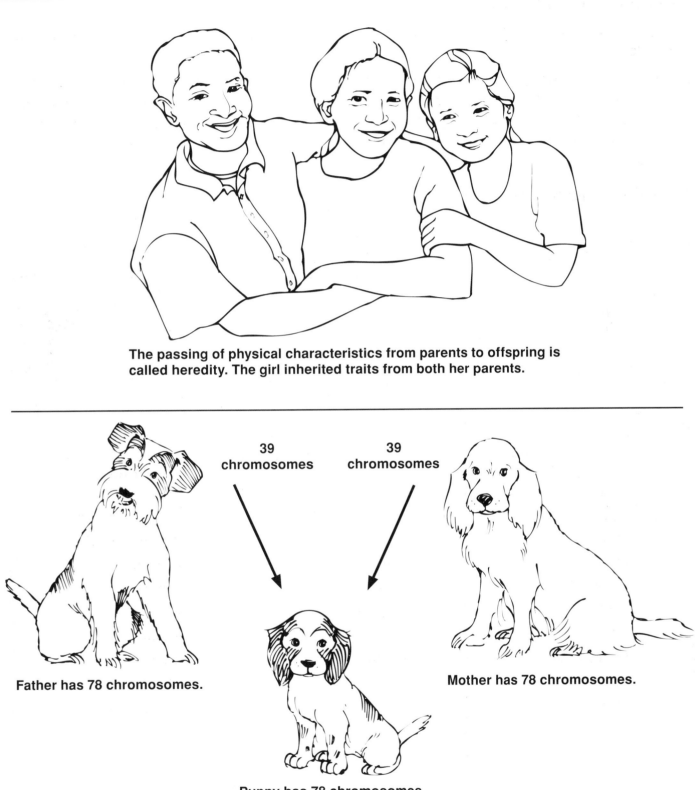

The passing of physical characteristics from parents to offspring is called heredity. The girl inherited traits from both her parents.

39 chromosomes

39 chromosomes

Father has 78 chromosomes.

Mother has 78 chromosomes.

Puppy has 78 chromosomes.

The genes on the chromosomes gave the puppy traits from its parents.

Family Traits

Children often look like their parents. Their traits are similar. A girl's eyes are brown, and so are her father's. A boy's hair is curly, just like his mother's. Have you ever wondered why?

Traits are physical features that make each person special. Traits are such things as hair color, eye color, and height. Children get traits from their parents. Some traits are from the mother. Other traits are from the father.

Parents' traits are passed on to babies. It happens before babies are born. It happens when they are first formed. The traits come from two tiny cells. One tiny cell comes from the mother. The other comes from the father.

Each tiny cell contains chromosomes. The chromosomes carry genes. Genes tell what traits will be passed on to the baby. The mother's chromosomes are in her tiny cell. These chromosomes have her genes. The father's chromosomes are in his tiny cell. These chromosomes have his genes.

The two tiny cells join. The mother's tiny cell joins the father's. A new cell is made, and it is called a body cell. The body cell has 46 chromosomes. Half, or 23, of the chromosomes are from the mother. Half, or 23, are from the father. The body cell is the start of a baby.

The body cell grows and becomes many cells. Soon, it's a baby. The baby is born with similar traits as the parents. The baby may have brown eyes, like the father. The baby may get curly hair, just like the mother.

The baby grows into a child. The child may develop features like the parents in many ways. The child may grow tall, like the father. The child may have dimples, like the mother.

But children don't look exactly like their parents. Each child is special!

Nonfiction Reading Practice, Grade 4 • EMC 3315 • ©2003 by Evan-Moor Corp.

Name _____

Family Traits

Fill in the bubble to answer each question or complete each sentence.

1. What does the word *traits* mean?
   - Ⓐ the way a baby grows into a child
   - Ⓑ the reason people look exactly alike
   - Ⓒ physical features that make each person special
   - Ⓓ special feelings parents have for their children

2. Where do children get traits?
   - Ⓐ from their parents
   - Ⓑ from babies
   - Ⓒ from their brothers and sisters
   - Ⓓ nobody knows

3. Traits come from two _____.
   - Ⓐ features
   - Ⓑ skin cells
   - Ⓒ large cells
   - Ⓓ tiny cells

4. Each tiny cell contains _____ that carry genes.
   - Ⓐ physical features
   - Ⓑ chromosomes
   - Ⓒ two more cells
   - Ⓓ body cells

5. Humans have _____ chromosomes in their body cells.
   - Ⓐ 2
   - Ⓑ 23
   - Ⓒ 46
   - Ⓓ 78

Bonus: On the back of this page, list five traits that people can have.

The Power of Chromosomes

Isn't it amazing that dogs always give birth to puppies? Dogs don't get mixed up and have kittens, chicks, or tadpoles. An animal always gives birth to the same kind of animal.

You might also notice that puppies usually look like their parents. They have similar traits. Some puppies might look like the mother dog. Some might look like the father. Some might look like a combination of both parents.

The same is true for people and plants. People give birth to people. Human babies usually have similar traits to their parents. And tomato plants produce tomato plants. The young plants have traits similar to the parent plants.

Animals and plants are made up of cells called body cells. The body cells of animals and plants contain chromosomes. Each type of animal or plant has a certain number of chromosomes in each body cell. All dogs have 78 chromosomes. All humans have 46 chromosomes. All tomato plants have 24 chromosomes.

Chromosomes are powerful. They tell the cell what to do. Chromosomes also carry genes. Genes determine traits like what color of fur a puppy will have, or what kind of hair a person will have, or how tall a tomato plant will be.

Animals and plants get their chromosomes from their two parents. An animal has a mother and a father. Plants also have two parents, similar to a mother and father. Half of an animal or plant's chromosomes come from its mother. These chromosomes carry the mother's genes. The other half comes from the father. These chromosomes carry his genes.

For a puppy, 39 chromosomes came from its mother and 39 from its father. That's a total of 78 chromosomes in the puppy's body cells. For the rest of the puppy's life, it will have 78 chromosomes in each body cell. These chromosomes make the animal grow into a dog. They also give the puppy traits from its parents.

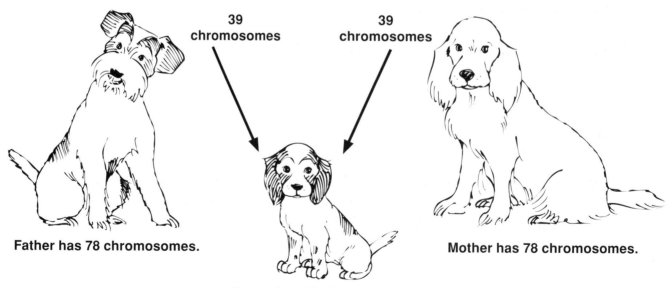

39 chromosomes

39 chromosomes

Father has 78 chromosomes.

Puppy has 78 chromosomes.

Mother has 78 chromosomes.

Nonfiction Reading Practice, Grade 4 • EMC 3315 • ©2003 by Evan-Moor Corp.

Name _____

The Power of Chromosomes

Fill in the bubble to answer each question or complete each sentence.

1. Puppies usually look like their parents because puppies have similar _____.
   - Ⓐ offspring
   - Ⓑ sizes
   - Ⓒ traits
   - Ⓓ tails

2. Animals and plants are made up of cells called _____.
   - Ⓐ body cells
   - Ⓑ skin cells
   - Ⓒ blood cells
   - Ⓓ nerve cells

3. Why are chromosomes so powerful?
   - Ⓐ There is the same number of chromosomes in every living thing.
   - Ⓑ They tell the body cells what to do.
   - Ⓒ They are in the body cells of plants.
   - Ⓓ They are in the body cells of animals.

4. Where do plants and animals get their chromosomes?
   - Ⓐ from their traits
   - Ⓑ from their two parents
   - Ⓒ from their offspring
   - Ⓓ from their brothers and sisters

5. How many chromosomes does a puppy have?
   - Ⓐ 24
   - Ⓑ 39
   - Ⓒ 46
   - Ⓓ 78

Bonus: Answer these questions on the back of this page: If people have 46 chromosomes, how many did they get from their mother? How many did they get from their father?

Mendel's Discovery

In 1857, Gregor Mendel decided to find out about heredity. *Heredity* is when traits, like hair and skin color, are passed from parents to their offspring. Heredity happens with people, animals, and plants.

In Mendel's time, people thought that when parents passed traits to their offspring, the traits mixed together. The mother's traits mixed with the father's, and the offspring was a mix of both parents. For example, a tall parent and a short parent would produce medium-height offspring. Were they right?

Mendel decided to find out. He experimented with pea plants. Some plants were tall, and some were short. When he bred two tall plants together, they produced tall offspring. Two short plants produced short offspring. Mendel wasn't surprised. He expected identical parents to produce plants like themselves.

Gregor Mendel

Mendel did a second experiment. He bred a tall plant with a short plant. He wondered if traits from the two different plants would mix together and produce medium-height plants. Mendel was amazed. The new plant was tall! Mendel realized that traits don't mix together. He also realized that some traits are stronger than others. In pea plants, the tall trait is stronger than the short.

Mendel did a third experiment. He bred together the new plants from the second experiment. He wasn't surprised to find tall plants. But he was amazed to find a few short ones! Mendel figured out that traits could pass from generation to generation. In some generations, they might be hidden by stronger traits.

Mendel also concluded that offspring get one kind of each trait from each parent. In the third experiment, some plants got a tall trait from both parents, so they produced tall offspring. Other plants got one tall trait and one short trait. They produced all tall plants because tall is a stronger trait. The shorter plants got a short trait from both parents. They produced short plants because no tall traits hid them.

Today, we know chromosomes are inside the cells of all plants and animals. Plant, animal, and human parents pass their chromosomes to their offspring. The genes in chromosomes determine the traits that are passed on from parent to child.

Name _____

Mendel's Discovery

Fill in the bubble to answer each question or complete each sentence.

1. What is *heredity*?
   - Ⓐ when traits are passed from parent to offspring
   - Ⓑ another word for *experiment*
   - Ⓒ a type of pea plant
   - Ⓓ something Mendel found inside the cells of a pea plant

2. What is an example of a trait?
   - Ⓐ a pea plant
   - Ⓑ a chromosome
   - Ⓒ a skin color
   - Ⓓ an animal

3. What did Mendel do?
   - Ⓐ He discovered pea plants.
   - Ⓑ He experimented with pea plants.
   - Ⓒ He named chromosomes.
   - Ⓓ He studied chromosomes under a microscope.

4. Mendel realized after his second experiment that _____.
   - Ⓐ all pea plants are tall
   - Ⓑ new plants contain chromosomes
   - Ⓒ only short plants were produced
   - Ⓓ traits don't mix together

5. Which is the stronger trait in pea plants?
   - Ⓐ a short trait
   - Ⓑ a tall trait
   - Ⓒ No traits are strong in a pea plant.
   - Ⓓ Both short and tall traits are strong.

Bonus: On the back of this page, explain why you think Mendel didn't talk about chromosomes when he did his experiments in 1857.

Measuring the Weather

Introducing the Topic

1. Reproduce page 63 for individual students, or make a transparency to use with a group or the whole class.

2. Show students the different simple instruments people use to measure the weather. Share with students that meteorologists study clouds, winds, and the temperature and pressure of Earth's atmosphere by using more sophisticated scientific instruments.

Reading the Selections

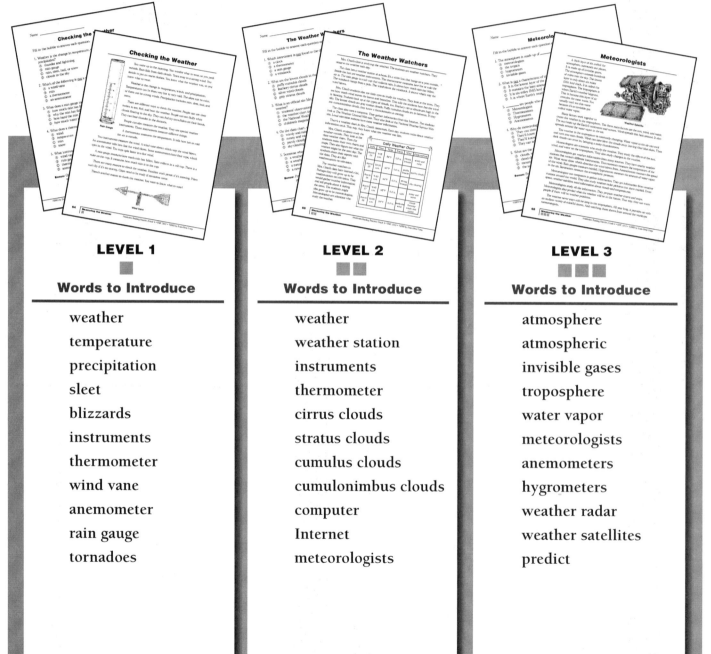

LEVEL 1

Words to Introduce

weather

temperature

precipitation

sleet

blizzards

instruments

thermometer

wind vane

anemometer

rain gauge

tornadoes

LEVEL 2

Words to Introduce

weather

weather station

instruments

thermometer

cirrus clouds

stratus clouds

cumulus clouds

cumulonimbus clouds

computer

Internet

meteorologists

LEVEL 3

Words to Introduce

atmosphere

atmospheric

invisible gases

troposphere

water vapor

meteorologists

anemometers

hygrometers

weather radar

weather satellites

predict

Weather Instruments

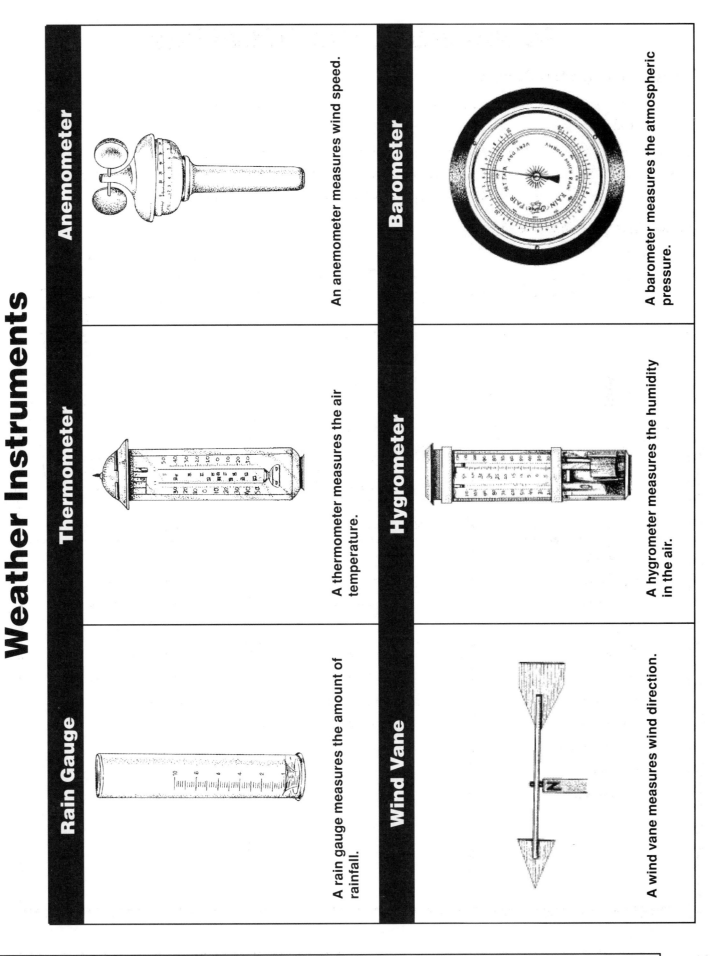

Anemometer

An anemometer measures wind speed.

Thermometer

A thermometer measures the air temperature.

Rain Gauge

A rain gauge measures the amount of rainfall.

Barometer

A barometer measures the atmospheric pressure.

Hygrometer

A hygrometer measures the humidity in the air.

Wind Vane

A wind vane measures wind direction.

Checking the Weather

You wake up in the morning. You wonder what to wear, so you peek outside. Rain falls from dark clouds. Trees sway in a strong wind. You decide to put on warm clothes. You knew what the weather was, so you knew what to wear.

Weather is the change in temperature, winds, and precipitation. Temperatures can be from very hot to very cold. The skies can be calm, or there can be strong winds. Precipitation includes rain, sleet, hail, and snow.

There are different ways to check the weather. People can use their bodies to see, feel, and hear the weather. People can see fluffy white clouds floating in the sky. They can feel icy snowflakes on their hands. They can hear thunder in the distance.

People can also measure the weather. They use special weather instruments. These instruments measure different things.

A thermometer measures the temperature. It tells how hot or cold the air is outside.

Two instruments measure the wind. A wind vane shows which way the wind blows. An anemometer tells how fast the wind blows. Some anemometers have four cups, which spin in the wind. The cups spin faster in a fast wind.

A rain gauge measures how much rain has fallen. Rain collects in a tall cup. There is a ruler on the cup. It measures how much rain is in the cup.

There are many reasons to check the weather. Families won't picnic if it's snowing. Pilots can't fly if it's too stormy. Cities need to be ready if tornadoes come.

There's another reason to check the weather. You want to know what to wear!

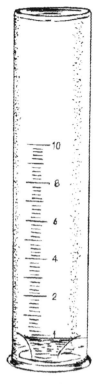

Rain Gauge

Wind Vane

Nonfiction Reading Practice, Grade 4 • EMC 3315 • ©2003 by Evan-Moor Corp.

Name _____

Checking the Weather

Fill in the bubble to answer each question.

1. Weather is the change in temperature, winds, and precipitation. What is *precipitation*?
   Ⓐ thunder and lightning
   Ⓑ rain gauge
   Ⓒ rain, sleet, hail, or snow
   Ⓓ clouds in the sky

2. Which of the following is not a weather instrument?
   Ⓐ a wind vane
   Ⓑ rain
   Ⓒ a thermometer
   Ⓓ an anemometer

3. What does a rain gauge measure?
   Ⓐ how much rain has fallen
   Ⓑ why the rain has fallen
   Ⓒ how hard the rain has fallen
   Ⓓ how much water is in a rain cloud

4. What does a thermometer measure?
   Ⓐ wind
   Ⓑ temperature
   Ⓒ rain
   Ⓓ snow

5. What instrument measures how fast the wind blows?
   Ⓐ wind vane
   Ⓑ rain gauge
   Ⓒ thermometer
   Ⓓ anemometer

Bonus: On the back of this page, give three reasons why people check the weather.

The Weather Watchers

Mrs. Chan's class is studying the weather. The students are weather watchers. They observe the weather each day.

The class has a weather station at school. It's a white box that hangs on a post outside. Inside the box are weather instruments. The thermometer measures how hot or cold the air is. The rain gauge is a tall cup that collects rain. It shows how much rain has fallen. The windsock hangs from a pole. The wind blows the windsock. It shows which way the wind blows.

Mrs. Chan's students also use their eyes to study the weather. They look at the trees. They see how much wind moves the leaves and branches. This tells the students how fast the wind is blowing. Students look up at the types of clouds, too. Feathery cirrus clouds are high in the sky. The lowest clouds are gray stratus clouds. Puffy cumulus clouds are in between. If they see cumulonimbus clouds, they know a thunderstorm is coming.

The class also uses a computer. They gather information from the Internet. The students look at The Weather Channel Web site. They also look at the National Weather Service Web site. Local television stations have more weather information.

There's a weather chart in Mrs. Chan's classroom. Each day, students write down weather information on it. This way, they know what the weather was like.

Mrs. Chan's students study the weather outside. They look at the class weather chart. Then the students make their own charts and maps. They also figure out what the weather might be the next day. The students share their reports with the class. They act like weathercasters on television.

The weather watchers in Mrs. Chan's class have learned a lot. Perhaps they will grow up to be weathercasters on television. They would gather weather information and tell people about it during the news. The students might also grow up to be meteorologists. Meteorologists are scientists who study the weather.

Daily Weather Chart

Date	Time	Temp	Precip	Wind	Observations
March 24	9:15 a.m.	56°F	0.5 in.	strong breeze	windy and rainy
March 25	10:00 a.m.	60°F	0.0 in.	gentle breeze	partly cloudy
March 26	9:30 a.m.	64°F	0.0 in.	strong breeze	sky clearing
March 27	9:45 a.m.	65°F	0.0 in.	calm	sunny and warm
March 28	10:00 a.m.	59°F	0.0 in.	moderate wind	clouds forming- windy and cooler

Name _____

The Weather Watchers

Fill in the bubble to answer each question or complete each sentence.

1. Which instrument is <u>not</u> found in the class weather station?
   - Ⓐ a clock
   - Ⓑ a thermometer
   - Ⓒ a rain gauge
   - Ⓓ a windsock

2. What are the lowest clouds in the sky?
   - Ⓐ puffy cumulus clouds
   - Ⓑ feathery cirrus clouds
   - Ⓒ silver wind clouds
   - Ⓓ gray stratus clouds

3. What is an official site Mrs. Chan's class can research to learn about the weather?
   - Ⓐ students' observations of the weather
   - Ⓑ the weather chart in the classroom
   - Ⓒ the National Weather Service Web site
   - Ⓓ children's magazines

4. On the class chart, what weather observations were made on March 27?
   - Ⓐ windy and rainy
   - Ⓑ sunny and warm
   - Ⓒ partly cloudy
   - Ⓓ sky clearing

5. Someone who studies weather is called _____.
   - Ⓐ a weather station
   - Ⓑ a weather report
   - Ⓒ a meteorologist
   - Ⓓ a newscaster

Bonus: Pretend you are a weather watcher. On the back of this page, list things you would report about today's weather.

Meteorologists

A thick layer of air, called the atmosphere, surrounds our planet. It is made up of invisible gases. The atmosphere extends hundreds of miles into the sky. The lowest layer is only about six miles (9.65 km) thick. It is called the troposphere. The troposphere is where Earth's weather happens. This is because this layer of air contains the most water. You usually can't see this water because it's an invisible gas called water vapor.

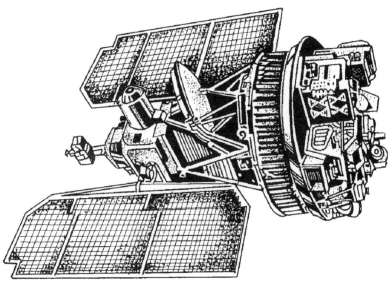

Weather Satellite

Many factors work together to create the weather in the troposphere. The three main factors are the sun, wind, and water. The sun heats up the Earth's continents and oceans. Wind spreads this heat around. It also spreads around the water vapor in the air.

The weather in the troposphere is constantly changing. Water vapor in the air can cool and turn into rain clouds. Wind can later blow the clouds away, leaving clear blue skies. Then dark clouds can scoot in, bringing a noisy thunderstorm.

Meteorologists are scientists who study the weather. They study the effects of the sun, wind, and water on the troposphere. They also study changes in the weather.

Meteorologists get weather information from many sources. They have nearby weather stations that contain different instruments. Thermometers measure the temperature of the air. Wind vanes show which direction the wind blows from. Anemometers measure the speed of the wind. Rain gauges measure rainfall. Hygrometers measure the amount of water vapor in the air. Barometers measure the atmospheric pressure.

Meteorologists use computers to gather information. They get information from weather stations around the world. They also study weather radar pictures that show rainfall. From space, weather satellites send information about clouds and temperatures.

Meteorologists study all the information. They prepare weather charts and maps. Meteorologists also predict what the weather will be in the future. That way, they can warn people if there will be weather problems.

The weather never stays still for long in the troposphere. All year long, it provides us with an endless variety of colorful shows. And watching those shows from around the world are meteorologists.

Nonfiction Reading Practice, Grade 4 • EMC 3315 • ©2003 by Evan-Moor Corp.

Name _____

Meteorologists

Fill in the bubble to answer each question or complete each sentence.

1. The atmosphere is made up of _____.
   - Ⓐ meteorologists
   - Ⓑ the tropics
   - Ⓒ hygrometers
   - Ⓓ invisible gases

2. What is <u>not</u> a characteristic of the troposphere?
   - Ⓐ It is the lowest layer of the atmosphere.
   - Ⓑ It contains the least amount of water vapor.
   - Ⓒ It is six miles (9.65 km) thick.
   - Ⓓ It is where Earth's weather happens.

3. _____ are people who study the weather.
   - Ⓐ Meteorologists
   - Ⓑ Thermometers
   - Ⓒ Hygrometers
   - Ⓓ Anemometers

4. Why do meteorologists get weather information from many sources?
   - Ⓐ They can then draw a map.
   - Ⓑ They'll know what the weather will be next week.
   - Ⓒ They'll know as much weather information as possible.
   - Ⓓ They can tell people what it is like to be a meteorologist.

5. What are the three main factors that work together to make weather?
   - Ⓐ clouds, wind, and snow
   - Ⓑ cloud charts, maps, and satellites
   - Ⓒ mountains, rivers, and grasses
   - Ⓓ the sun, wind, and water

Bonus: Pretend you're a meteorologist. On the back of this page, name and define four instruments you would use to find out about the weather today.

The Internet

Introducing the Topic

1. Reproduce page 71 for individual students, or make a transparency to use with a group or the whole class.

2. Show students the diagrams, and discuss how the Internet works. Ask students what kinds of things they like to do on the Internet. Explain that almost everyone uses the Internet today, but it hasn't always been around.

Reading the Selections

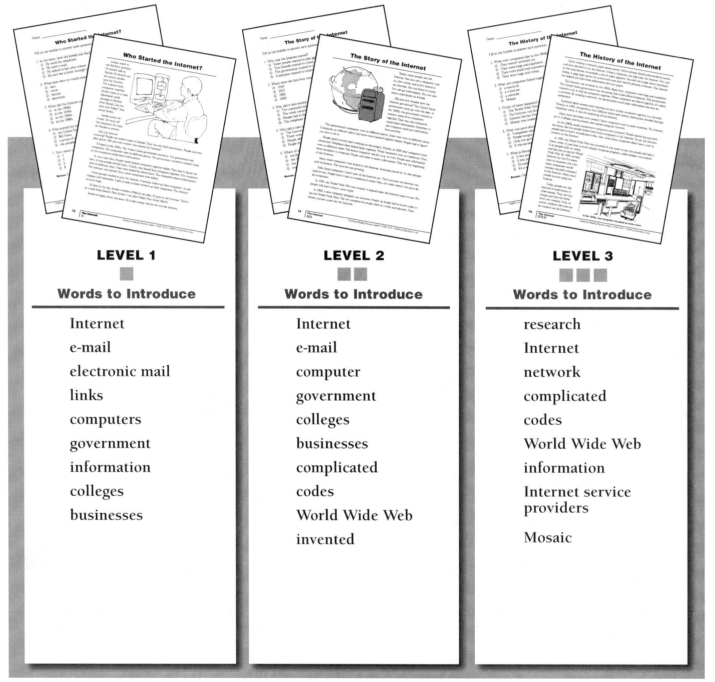

LEVEL 1	LEVEL 2	LEVEL 3
Words to Introduce	**Words to Introduce**	**Words to Introduce**
Internet	Internet	research
e-mail	e-mail	Internet
electronic mail	computer	network
links	government	complicated
computers	colleges	codes
government	businesses	World Wide Web
information	complicated	information
colleges	codes	Internet service providers
businesses	World Wide Web	Mosaic
	invented	

Nonfiction Reading Practice, Grade 4 • EMC 3315 • ©2003 by Evan-Moor Corp.

How the Internet Works

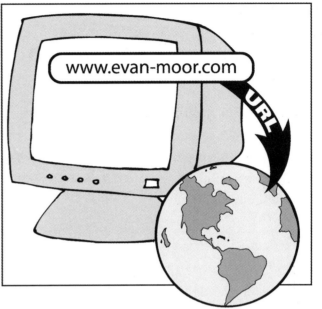

1. To get onto a Web site, you first enter its address, called a URL (Uniform Resource Locator), in the address box of your browser.

2. Your Web browser sends your request to a Web server located at your ISP (Internet Service Provider).

3. The Web server finds the files, then downloads them to your computer.

4. Your Web browser puts the page together on your screen. Now you are ready to read the information.

Who Started the Internet?

Jordan wants to ask Rachel a question. He doesn't talk to Rachel. He doesn't use the phone. Jordan uses the Internet. The Internet links computers together. Jordan types an e-mail (electronic mail) message to Rachel: *Dear Rachel, Can you come over Friday? Your friend, Jordan.*

Jordan sends the e-mail. He turns off the computer. He waits for Rachel to answer.

Isn't the Internet amazing? People can send e-mails to friends. They can also find information. People can even play games. Did you ever wonder who started the Internet?

It began in the 1960s. The United States government started it. The government had computers. The computers were in different places. The government wanted to connect them so the computers could share information.

It was a new idea. People hadn't linked computers together before. They had to figure out how. It took people several years. Finally, they joined four computers together. The computers were in different cities. They were linked by phone lines. The computers shared information. The Internet was started. Soon, more computers were added.

Other groups wanted to join the Internet. Scientists linked up their computers. So did colleges and businesses. Later, people at home hooked up their computers. The Internet became huge.

It's later in the day. Jordan wonders if Rachel can play. He gets on the Internet. There's an e-mail from Rachel: *Dear Jordan, I can play Friday! Your friend, Rachel.*

Jordan is happy about the news. He is also happy that he can use the Internet.

Nonfiction Reading Practice, Grade 4 • EMC 3315 • ©2003 by Evan-Moor Corp.

Name _____

Who Started the Internet?

Fill in the bubble to answer each question.

1. In the story, how did Jordan ask Rachel a question?
   - Ⓐ He used the telephone.
   - Ⓑ He used e-mail.
   - Ⓒ He talked to her after school.
   - Ⓓ He sent her a letter through the mail.

2. What does the *e* in *e-mail* mean?
   - Ⓐ easy
   - Ⓑ extra
   - Ⓒ electric
   - Ⓓ electronic

3. When did the Internet start?
   - Ⓐ in the 1890s
   - Ⓑ in the 1940s
   - Ⓒ in the 1960s
   - Ⓓ in the 1980s

4. Who started the Internet?
   - Ⓐ the United States government
   - Ⓑ Bill Gates
   - Ⓒ a group of teachers
   - Ⓓ the president of the United States

5. How many computers were first joined together?
   - Ⓐ 3
   - Ⓑ 4
   - Ⓒ 6
   - Ⓓ 8

Bonus: On the back of this page, explain why the Internet was first started.

The Story of the Internet

Today, many people use the Internet. You turn on a computer, type in a few words, and you're linked to the Internet. You can listen to music. You can get information. You can also send e-mail letters to friends.

Did you ever wonder how the Internet got started? The United States government came up with the idea. In the 1960s, the government wanted to connect some of its computers together. That way, the computers could share information. Someone on one computer could get information from another.

The government's computers were in different places. Some were even in different states. Computers in different places had never been hooked together before. People had to figure out how to do it.

People spent several years working on the project. Finally, in 1969, four computers were connected. Telephone lines linked them together. Three computers were in California. They were in different cities. The fourth computer was far away in Utah. People sent information from computer to computer. People were able to share information. This was the beginning of the Internet.

Many more computers were linked to the Internet. Scientists joined in. So did colleges and businesses. The Internet was growing.

Still, home computers weren't part of the Internet yet. That's because the Internet was hard to use. People had to type in complicated codes. Also, the codes weren't the same for all computers.

In 1991, the World Wide Web was created. It helped make the Internet easier to use. But people still had to know some codes.

In 1992, a new computer program was invented. People no longer had to know codes to use the World Wide Web. The new program let people click on words and pictures. Then almost anyone could use the Internet.

Nonfiction Reading Practice, Grade 4 • EMC 3315 • ©2003 by Evan-Moor Corp.

Name _____

The Story of the Internet

Fill in the bubble to answer each question.

1. Why was the Internet started?
   - Ⓐ Some people wanted to play games with other people on their computers.
   - Ⓑ Two friends wanted to e-mail each other.
   - Ⓒ The government wanted to connect its computers together.
   - Ⓓ A scientist wanted to communicate with other scientists.

2. When were the first four computers connected together?
   - Ⓐ 1950
   - Ⓑ 1955
   - Ⓒ 1962
   - Ⓓ 1969

3. Why did it take several years to link the four computers together?
   - Ⓐ The computers kept breaking down.
   - Ⓑ The wires weren't long enough to go from room to room.
   - Ⓒ People had to figure out how to hook them together.
   - Ⓓ The telephone lines had to be put up on electric poles.

4. Why did it take so long to hook home computers to the Internet?
   - Ⓐ The Internet was hard to use at first.
   - Ⓑ There weren't enough computers.
   - Ⓒ People didn't have enough money.
   - Ⓓ People lived too far from the government.

5. Which of these was created in 1991?
   - Ⓐ the first computer
   - Ⓑ the World Wide Web
   - Ⓒ the Internet
   - Ⓓ e-mail

Bonus: On the back of this page, list at least four things people can use the Internet for today.

The History of the Internet

You're writing a research paper about horses. You've already found information in books, and have decided to try the Internet. Using a computer, you sign onto the Internet. You type in the word *horses*. In seconds, a list of topics appears. You click on a topic about horseback riding. A page pops up on the screen with text and colorful pictures of horses. The Internet has helped you find more information for your paper.

The Internet was invented in the 1960s. Back then, computers were huge and expensive. The United States government was one group that could afford computers. The government wanted a way to link its computers together. When computers are linked together, it's called a network. By creating a network, the government could share information between its computers.

Scientists spent several years figuring out how to link computers together in a network. Finally, in 1969, computers in four different cities were linked. Information traveled through telephone wires. It was the beginning of the Internet.

Soon, more networks were created. Some computers were in other countries. The Internet grew. Colleges and businesses also started using the Internet.

In the 1980s, small, inexpensive computers were invented. People started buying them for home. But few people linked their home computers to the Internet. To use the Internet, people had to know complicated codes. Also, most home computers didn't have a way to connect to the Internet.

In 1991, the World Wide Web was invented. It was easier to use, but people still had to know codes. A year later, a much simpler computer program, called Mosaic, was created. It let people click on words and pictures to use the World Wide Web. By 1995, several Internet Service Providers were in business. For a fee, these companies would connect anyone's computer to the Internet. Many more people started using the Internet.

Today, people use the Internet to send letters to other people. They can buy things and find out about news and weather. And, of course, students like you can do research on the Internet.

In the 1960s, one computer occupied an entire room.

Nonfiction Reading Practice, Grade 4 • EMC 3315 • ©2003 by Evan-Moor Corp.

Name _____

The History of the Internet

Fill in the bubble to answer each question.

1. What were computers like in the 1960s?
   - Ⓐ They weren't invented yet.
   - Ⓑ They were huge and expensive.
   - Ⓒ They were small and expensive.
   - Ⓓ They were huge and cheap.

2. What are computers linked together called?
   - Ⓐ a match-fit
   - Ⓑ a wired set
   - Ⓒ a network
   - Ⓓ Mosaic

3. Which of these happened in 1991?
   - Ⓐ The World Wide Web was invented.
   - Ⓑ The Internet was first started.
   - Ⓒ Internet Service Providers first started.
   - Ⓓ Mosaic was created.

4. What was good about the World Wide Web?
   - Ⓐ Companies made more expensive computers.
   - Ⓑ People bought computers.
   - Ⓒ Only the government could use the World Wide Web.
   - Ⓓ It was an easier way for more people to use the Internet.

5. What is Mosaic?
   - Ⓐ It lets people create artwork on the Internet.
   - Ⓑ It lets people click on words and pictures while using the Internet.
   - Ⓒ It's another name for the Internet.
   - Ⓓ It's a way to network several computers together at home.

Bonus: On the back of this page, explain why the Internet was a good invention.

Marie Curie

Introducing the Topic

1. Reproduce page 79 for individual students, or make a transparency to use with a group or the whole class.

2. Show students the time line of Marie Curie. Point out the dates and her accomplishments. Remind students that she was a pioneer in the field of science.

Reading the Selections

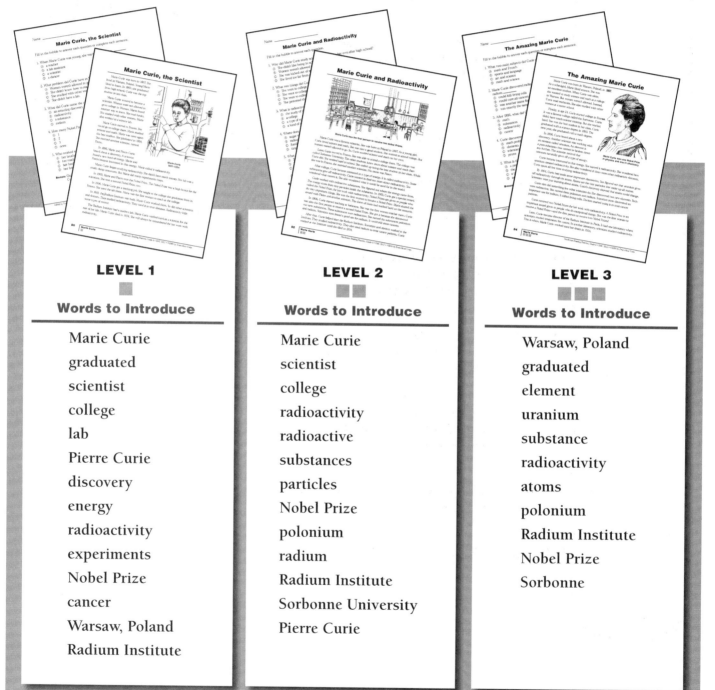

LEVEL 1 ■	LEVEL 2 ■ ■	LEVEL 3 ■ ■ ■
Words to Introduce	**Words to Introduce**	**Words to Introduce**
Marie Curie	Marie Curie	Warsaw, Poland
graduated	scientist	graduated
scientist	college	element
college	radioactivity	uranium
lab	radioactive	substance
Pierre Curie	substances	radioactivity
discovery	particles	atoms
energy	Nobel Prize	polonium
radioactivity	polonium	Radium Institute
experiments	radium	Nobel Prize
Nobel Prize	Radium Institute	Sorbonne
cancer	Sorbonne University	
Warsaw, Poland	Pierre Curie	
Radium Institute		

Nonfiction Reading Practice, Grade 4 • EMC 3315 • ©2003 by Evan-Moor Corp.

Time Line of Marie Curie

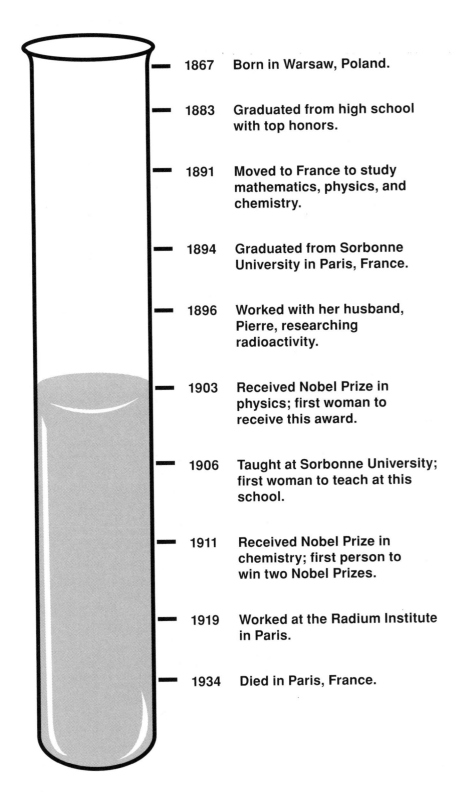

1867   Born in Warsaw, Poland.

1883   Graduated from high school with top honors.

1891   Moved to France to study mathematics, physics, and chemistry.

1894   Graduated from Sorbonne University in Paris, France.

1896   Worked with her husband, Pierre, researching radioactivity.

1903   Received Nobel Prize in physics; first woman to receive this award.

1906   Taught at Sorbonne University; first woman to teach at this school.

1911   Received Nobel Prize in chemistry; first person to win two Nobel Prizes.

1919   Worked at the Radium Institute in Paris.

1934   Died in Paris, France.

Marie Curie, the Scientist

Marie Curie was born in 1867. She lived in Warsaw, Poland. Young Marie liked to learn. In 1883, she graduated from high school. Curie was the top student in her class.

Marie Curie wanted to become a scientist. Women were not allowed to go to college in Warsaw. Marie found another way to learn. She read books. She studied with other women. Marie also worked in a science lab.

Marie Curie moved to France. She could go to college there. Marie studied science and math. Marie was once again the best student. She graduated in 1894. She married another scientist, named Pierre.

In 1896, Marie and Pierre Curie heard about a discovery. A scientist found a new kind of energy. Marie and Pierre became interested in this energy. Marie called it radioactivity.

**Marie Curie
1867–1934**

Marie Curie began studying radioactivity. She didn't have much money. Her lab was a small, damp storeroom. But Marie did many experiments there.

In 1903, Marie and Pierre won the Nobel Prize. The Nobel Prize was a high honor for the scientists. She won a second Nobel Prize, too.

In 1906, Marie Curie got a teaching job. She taught at the college she graduated from in France. She used the lab there. Marie was the first woman to teach at the college.

In 1919, the Radium Institute was built. Marie Curie worked there. So did other scientists and doctors. They studied radioactivity. They used it to treat diseases. Radioactivity kills some types of cancer.

The Radium Institute had a modern lab. Marie Curie worked hard as a scientist for the rest of her life. Marie Curie died in 1934. She will always be remembered for her work with radioactivity.

Nonfiction Reading Practice, Grade 4 • EMC 3315 • ©2003 by Evan-Moor Corp.

Name _____

Marie Curie, the Scientist

Fill in the bubble to answer each question or complete each sentence.

1. When Marie Curie was young, she wanted to become _____.
   - Ⓐ a teacher
   - Ⓑ a lab assistant
   - Ⓒ a scientist
   - Ⓓ a dancer

2. What problem did Curie have in Warsaw?
   - Ⓐ Women weren't allowed to go to college.
   - Ⓑ She didn't know how to read.
   - Ⓒ She studied with other woman.
   - Ⓓ She didn't have a lab.

3. What did Curie name the new kind of energy?
   - Ⓐ an amazing discovery
   - Ⓑ radioactivity
   - Ⓒ a substance
   - Ⓓ radium

4. How many Nobel Prizes did Marie Curie receive?
   - Ⓐ 1
   - Ⓑ 2
   - Ⓒ 3
   - Ⓓ none

5. Who worked with Marie Curie in her lab?
   - Ⓐ her brother
   - Ⓑ her teacher
   - Ⓒ her husband
   - Ⓓ her friend

Bonus: On the back of this page, write two sentences that tell about Marie Curie.

Marie Curie and Radioactivity

Marie Curie was the first person to receive two Nobel Prizes.

Marie Curie was a famous scientist. She was born in Poland in 1867. As a young girl, Curie loved science and math. She was also a good student. She wanted to attend college. But women weren't allowed to go. So, Curie studied science and math on her own.

Later, Curie moved to France. She was able to attend a college there. The college was called Sorbonne University. The other students knew more about science and math than Curie did. She worked hard in school. She ended up being the best student in her class. While she was in France, she married another scientist. His name was Pierre.

After college, Curie became interested in a type of energy. It is called radioactivity. Some substances give off radioactivity. Curie wanted to find out more about radioactivity. She wondered what caused it. She also wondered what it could be used for in the world.

Curie worked with radioactive substances. She figured out where the energy came from. The energy came from tiny particles inside the substance. In 1903, Curie got a special award, called the Nobel Prize, for her work with radioactivity. Nobel Prizes are given to people who do very important things. She was the first woman to receive a Nobel Prize. Marie shared the award with Pierre and another scientist. The three of them had worked hard on the research.

In 1906, Curie started teaching at Sorbonne. She was the first woman teacher there. Curie was also the first person to receive a second Nobel Prize. She got it because she discovered two new substances. These substances were radioactive. She named the substances polonium and radium. Scientists soon found a good use for radium. It could kill some cancers.

After that, Curie helped start the Radium Institute. Scientists and doctors worked at the Institute. They studied radioactivity. They also used radium to treat cancer patients. Curie worked at the Institute until she died in 1934.

Nonfiction Reading Practice, Grade 4 • EMC 3315 • ©2003 by Evan-Moor Corp.

Name _____

Marie Curie and Radioactivity

Fill in the bubble to answer each question.

1. Why did Marie Curie study science and math on her own after high school?
   - Ⓐ She didn't like being in school.
   - Ⓑ Women weren't allowed in college.
   - Ⓒ She was kicked out of school.
   - Ⓓ She lived too far from college.

2. What two things did Curie do at Sorbonne University?
   - Ⓐ She went to college there and later taught at the university.
   - Ⓑ She went to college and married Pierre.
   - Ⓒ She went to college there but was unable to graduate.
   - Ⓓ She protested that women could not attend that college.

3. What is *radioactivity*?
   - Ⓐ the study of lively music
   - Ⓑ a college
   - Ⓒ a type of energy
   - Ⓓ a kind of science

4. Where does the energy from radioactivity come from?
   - Ⓐ sugar water
   - Ⓑ radium that is shot at a substance
   - Ⓒ fossils, shells, and old rocks
   - Ⓓ tiny particles inside a substance

5. What is one thing Curie did <u>not</u> do?
   - Ⓐ She was the first woman to get a Nobel Prize.
   - Ⓑ She was the first person to receive two Nobel Prizes.
   - Ⓒ She was the first person to discover that uranium gives off a type of energy.
   - Ⓓ She was the first woman to teach at the Sorbonne.

Bonus: On the back of this page, write three important "firsts" Marie Curie accomplished in her lifetime.

The Amazing Marie Curie

Marie Curie was born in Warsaw, Poland, in 1867. As a schoolgirl, Marie liked science. She was an excellent student. When Curie was older, she wanted to study science and math at a college in Warsaw. But women weren't allowed. Instead, Curie read textbooks. She also studied with other women at a secret school.

Finally, at age 24, Curie started college in France. It was a famous college called the Sorbonne. Curie didn't have much science training. But she worked hard. She was the best student in her class. Curie graduated with a science degree in 1893. The next year, she graduated with a math degree.

In 1896, Curie heard about a new discovery. Another scientist was working with an element called uranium. An element is a pure substance that cannot be broken down any further. The scientist noticed that uranium naturally gives off a type of energy.

Marie Curie won one Nobel Prize in physics and one in chemistry.

Curie became interested in this energy. She named it radioactivity. She wondered how uranium created radioactivity. She also wondered if there were other radioactive elements. Curie spent all her time studying radioactivity.

By 1904, Curie had made some important discoveries. She figured out that uranium gives off radioactivity through its atoms. Atoms are the tiny particles that make up all matter. Scientists were just learning about atoms. Curie's discovery showed that atoms could change.

Curie also did something few other scientists do. She discovered two new elements. Both were radioactive. She named them polonium and radium. Scientists soon discovered an important use for radium. It killed living cells. Doctors started using it to treat cancer patients.

Curie received two Nobel Prizes for her work with radioactivity. A Nobel Prize is an important award given to people who do exceptional things. She was the first woman to receive a Nobel Prize—and the first person to receive two Nobel Prizes!

Later, Curie became director of the Radium Institute in Paris. It had one laboratory where scientists studied treatments for cancer. In another laboratory, scientists studied radioactivity. This is where Marie Curie worked until her death in 1934.

Nonfiction Reading Practice, Grade 4 • EMC 3315 • ©2003 by Evan-Moor Corp.

Name _____

The Amazing Marie Curie

Fill in the bubble to answer each question or complete each sentence.

1. What two main subjects did Curie study in school?
   - Ⓐ math and French
   - Ⓑ sports and language
   - Ⓒ art and science
   - Ⓓ math and science

2. Marie Curie discovered radium. After that, scientists discovered that radium _____.
   - Ⓐ could kill living cells
   - Ⓑ could cure all cancers
   - Ⓒ was another name for uranium
   - Ⓓ was exactly the same element as polonium

3. After 1896, what did Curie study most of the time?
   - Ⓐ math
   - Ⓑ substances
   - Ⓒ radioactivity
   - Ⓓ cancer

4. Curie discovered two new _____.
   - Ⓐ math problems
   - Ⓑ elements
   - Ⓒ scientists
   - Ⓓ prizes

5. What is the Nobel Prize?
   - Ⓐ a present for a scientist
   - Ⓑ the name of a book that Curie wrote explaining radioactivity
   - Ⓒ a trophy given to scientists who take an important test
   - Ⓓ an award given to people who do exceptional things

Bonus: On the back of this page, write a paragraph about why people are amazed with the accomplishments of Marie Curie.

Teeth

Introducing the Topic

1. Reproduce page 87 for individual students, or make a transparency to use with a group or the whole class.

2. Tell students that people have two sets of teeth: primary and secondary. Show them the illustrations of the two sets of teeth. Discuss the eruption and shedding process and that the ages when these two things happen are just averages.

Reading the Selections

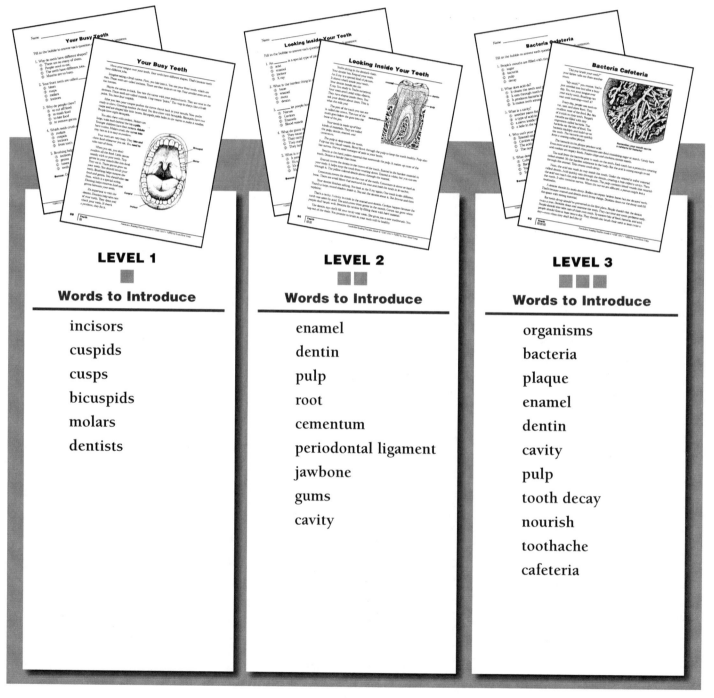

LEVEL 1

Words to Introduce

incisors

cuspids

cusps

bicuspids

molars

dentists

LEVEL 2

Words to Introduce

enamel

dentin

pulp

root

cementum

periodontal ligament

jawbone

gums

cavity

LEVEL 3

Words to Introduce

organisms

bacteria

plaque

enamel

dentin

cavity

pulp

tooth decay

nourish

toothache

cafeteria

Nonfiction Reading Practice, Grade 4 • EMC 3315 • ©2003 by Evan-Moor Corp.

Your Two Sets of Teeth

Primary Teeth of a Child

Upper

	Eruption (average age given)	Shedding (average age given)
Central incisor	7 1/2 months	7 1/2 years
Lateral incisor	9 months	8 years
Cuspid	18 months	11 1/2 years
First molar	14 months	10 1/2 years
Second molar	24 months	10 1/2 years

Second molar	20 months	11 years
First molar	12 months	10 years
Cuspid	16 months	9 1/2 years
Lateral incisor	7 months	7 years
Central incisor	6 months	6 years

Lower

Secondary Teeth of an Adult

Upper

	Shedding
Central incisor	7–8 years
Lateral incisor	8–9 years
Cuspid	11–12 years
First bicuspid	10–11 years
Second bicuspid	10–12 years
First molar	6–7 years
Second molar	12–13 years
Third molar	17–21 years
Third molar	17–21 years
Second molar	11–13 years
First molar	6–7 years
Second bicuspid	11–12 years
First bicuspid	10–12 years
Cuspid	9–10 years
Lateral incisor	7–8 years
Central incisor	6–7 years

Lower

Your Busy Teeth

Move your tongue over your teeth. Your teeth have different shapes. That's because teeth have different jobs.

Imagine eating a fresh carrot. First, you bite into it. You use your front teeth, which are thin. These teeth are called incisors. There are four incisors on top. Four smaller ones are on the bottom.

Maybe the carrot is thick. You bite the carrot with your pointed teeth. They are next to the incisors. These teeth are called cuspids. *Cusp* means "point." The cusp is sharp, like a knife point. You have four cuspids.

After you bite, your tongue pushes the carrot chunk back in your mouth. Now you're ready to chew. Chewing mashes the food. You first chew with bicuspids. Bicuspids have two cusps and are shaped like little boxes. Bicuspids poke holes in the carrot to make it smaller. People have eight bicuspids.

You also chew with molars. Molars are large, wide teeth behind the bicuspids. Younger children have four molars. Adults have twelve. Molars crush the carrot into tiny bits so it is easy to swallow.

Your teeth are very busy. They bite and chew food whenever you eat. You need to take care of them.

When you eat, you don't swallow all the food. Little pieces usually stick to your teeth. Tiny germs in your mouth like this food. They eat it. These germs grow on your teeth. You should brush your teeth. Brushing helps remove the food and germs. You should also use floss, which is a special string. Flossing helps removes food and germs between your teeth.

It's important to visit the dentist. Dentists help take care of your teeth. They clean and check your teeth. If there's a problem, they fix it.

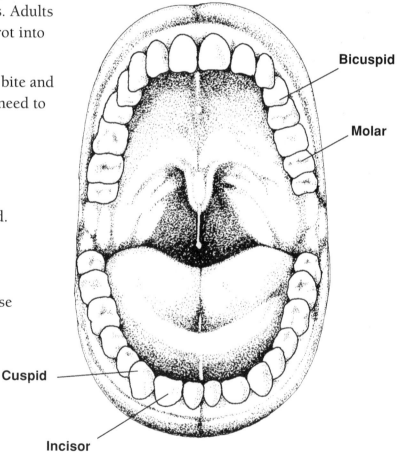

Bicuspid

Molar

Cuspid

Incisor

Nonfiction Reading Practice, Grade 4 • EMC 3315 • ©2003 by Evan-Moor Corp.

Name _____

Your Busy Teeth

Fill in the bubble to answer each question or complete each sentence.

1. Why do teeth have different shapes?
   - Ⓐ There are so many of them.
   - Ⓑ People need to eat.
   - Ⓒ The teeth have different jobs.
   - Ⓓ Mouths are so busy.

2. Your front teeth are called _____.
   - Ⓐ biters
   - Ⓑ cusps
   - Ⓒ molars
   - Ⓓ incisors

3. Why do people chew?
   - Ⓐ to cut off food
   - Ⓑ to mash food
   - Ⓒ to bite food
   - Ⓓ to remove germs

4. Which teeth crush a carrot into tiny bits so the carrot is easy to swallow?
   - Ⓐ molars
   - Ⓑ cuspids
   - Ⓒ incisors
   - Ⓓ front teeth

5. Brushing help removes food and _____.
   - Ⓐ incisors
   - Ⓑ germs
   - Ⓒ boxes
   - Ⓓ teeth

Bonus: On the back of this page, write two reasons to go to the dentist.

Looking Inside Your Teeth

You're sitting in the dentist's chair. Your dentist has X-rayed your teeth. An X ray is a special kind of picture. It shows what's inside your teeth. Your dentist hands you the X ray. You study it. You're surprised. Your teeth aren't solid white objects. They have shapes inside them. You ask your dentist about them. This is what she tells you:

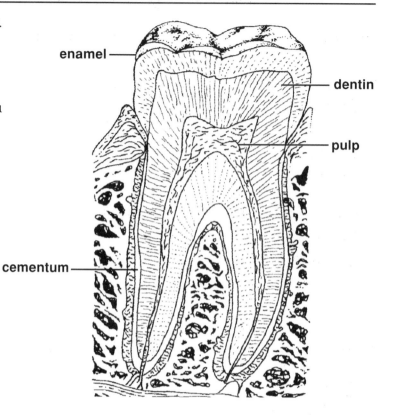

The part of the tooth you can see is called the crown. The root of the tooth goes below the gum into the bone of the jaw.

Your tooth is made up of four kinds of materials. They are called the pulp, dentin, enamel, and cementum.

The pulp is deep inside the tooth. Pulp has tiny blood vessels. Blood flows through the pulp to keep the tooth healthy. Pulp also has nerves. Nerves send messages of pain to your brain.

Dentin is the hard, yellow material that surrounds the pulp. It makes up most of the tooth. Dentin is harder than bone.

Enamel covers the dentin in the crown of the tooth. Enamel is the hardest material in your body. It helps keep the tooth from wearing down. Enamel is white, but you can see through it. The yellow colored dentin shows through the enamel.

Cementum covers the dentin in the root of the tooth. Cementum is about as hard as bone. There are small fibers that surround the root and hold the tooth in its socket.

Your dentist finishes talking. You look at the X ray again. One tooth looks different. There's a large, round shadow inside it. You ask the dentist about it. She frowns and then explains:

That's a cavity. A cavity is a hole in the enamel and dentin. Cavities happen because the tooth was eaten by acid. The acid comes from germs in the mouth. Germs can grow when people don't brush well. Dentists fix cavities by filling them with hard material.

The dentist says she'll fill your cavity next week. She gives you a new toothbrush. You hop out of the chair. You promise to brush so your teeth will be healthy.

Nonfiction Reading Practice, Grade 4 • EMC 3315 • ©2003 by Evan-Moor Corp.

Name _____

Looking Inside Your Teeth

Fill in the bubble to answer each question or complete each sentence

1. An _____ is a special type of picture.
   - (A) acid
   - (B) enamel
   - (C) incisor
   - (D) X ray

2. What is the hardest thing in the body?
   - (A) bone
   - (B) enamel
   - (C) roots
   - (D) dentin

3. _____ let people know how their teeth feel.
   - (A) Nerves
   - (B) Cavities
   - (C) Enamels
   - (D) Blood vessels

4. What do gums do?
   - (A) They cause cavities.
   - (B) They carry blood to your teeth.
   - (C) They make cementum inside the teeth.
   - (D) They help hold the teeth in place.

5. What is a *cavity*?
   - (A) It protects the tooth and gums.
   - (B) It's a type of germ.
   - (C) It's a hole in the enamel and dentin.
   - (D) It's the main part of a tooth.

Bonus: On the back of this page, write two reasons why people should brush
their teeth.

Bacteria Cafeteria

"Did you brush your teeth?" your father calls out from another room.

"My teeth?" you mutter. You've just crawled into bed after a busy day. You run your tongue over your sticky teeth. Brushing can wait until morning—can't it?

Every day, people use teeth to cut, tear, and chew food. They swallow most of the food. But bits of it stick to their teeth. People's mouths are filled with tiny organisms called bacteria. The bacteria eat the bits of food. The bacteria multiply and build up on the teeth. The bacteria can quickly form a coating called plaque.

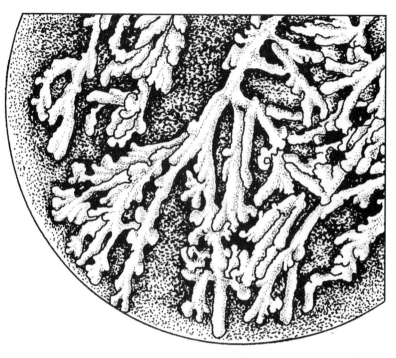

Remember, your mouth can be a cafeteria for bacteria!

The bacteria in the plaque produce acid. Even more acid is created when someone eats food containing sugar or starch. Candy bars and cookies are sugary foods. Potato chips and crackers contain starch.

The acid from the bacteria goes to work on the teeth. Each tooth has a protective covering called enamel. It's the hardest substance in the body. But the acid is strong enough to eat through the enamel. This creates tooth decay.

Next, the acid can work its way inside the tooth. Under the enamel is softer material called dentin. Acid quickly eats through the dentin, creating a hole called a cavity. Then the acid can reach the pulp inside the dentin. The pulp contains blood vessels that nourish the tooth. It also contains nerves. When the nerves are affected, a person might feel a toothache.

A dentist should fix tooth decay. Bodies can repair broken bones but not decayed teeth. That's because enamel and dentin aren't living things. Dentists clean out the decay and fill the space with strong material.

But tooth decay should be prevented in the first place. People should visit the dentist twice a year. Dentists clean and examine the teeth. They can treat any tooth problems early. People should also take care of their own teeth. To remove bits of food, bacteria, and acid, people should floss at least once a day. They should also brush their teeth at least twice a day—even when they don't feel like it!

Nonfiction Reading Practice, Grade 4 • EMC 3315 • ©2003 by Evan-Moor Corp.

Bacteria Cafeteria

Fill in the bubble to answer each question or complete each sentence.

1. People's mouths are filled with tiny organisms called _____.
   - Ⓐ sugar
   - Ⓑ bacteria
   - Ⓒ pulp
   - Ⓓ decay

2. What does acid do?
   - Ⓐ It cleans the teeth and protects them.
   - Ⓑ It eats through tooth enamel.
   - Ⓒ It produces bacteria in the mouth.
   - Ⓓ It makes teeth stronger.

3. What is a *cavity*?
   - Ⓐ another name for a dentist
   - Ⓑ a type of acid in people's mouths
   - Ⓒ a nerve inside the tooth
   - Ⓓ a hole in the tooth

4. Why can't your body repair decayed teeth?
   - Ⓐ Enamel and dentin aren't living things.
   - Ⓑ Cavities are too hard to fix.
   - Ⓒ The acid eats through the dentin.
   - Ⓓ The nerves are affected.

5. What does the title "Bacteria Cafeteria" mean?
   - Ⓐ Cafeterias serve food, and you chew food.
   - Ⓑ *Bacteria* and *cafeteria* rhyme.
   - Ⓒ Your mouth is like a cafeteria where bacteria can grow.
   - Ⓓ You eat in a cafeteria, and it has a lot of bacteria growing there.

Bonus: Imagine that someone has told you they rarely brush their teeth. On the back of this page, write a paragraph about the things you would tell that person about why brushing their teeth is important.

Seat Belt Safety

Introducing the Topic

1. Reproduce page 95 for individual students, or make a transparency to use with a group or the whole class.

2. Show students the illustration. Ask them what is wrong with the picture (people aren't wearing seat belts). Have students draw seat belts on the passengers in the picture. Have them use the model at the bottom of the page for reference. Discuss reasons why people might not wear seat belts.

Reading the Selections

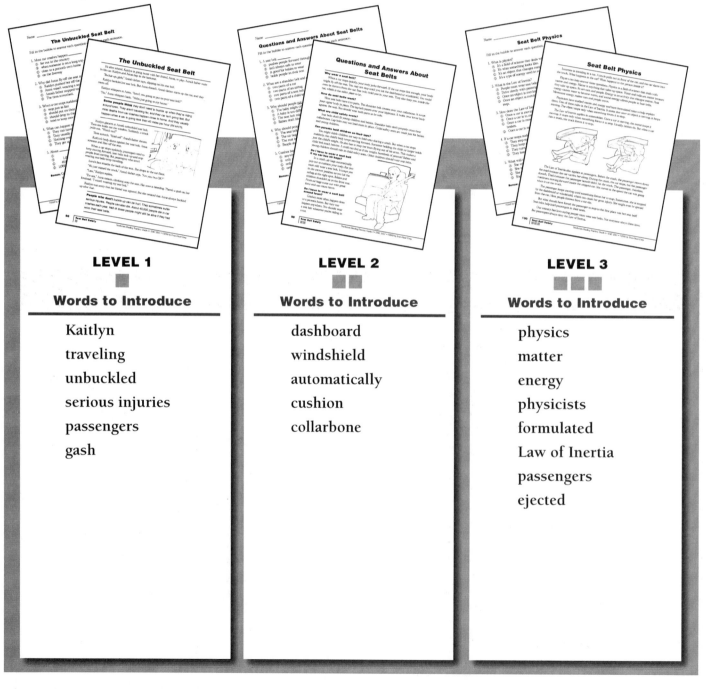

LEVEL 1	LEVEL 2	LEVEL 3
■	■ ■	■ ■ ■
Words to Introduce	**Words to Introduce**	**Words to Introduce**
Kaitlyn	dashboard	physics
traveling	windshield	matter
unbuckled	automatically	energy
serious injuries	cushion	physicists
passengers	collarbone	formulated
gash		Law of Inertia
		passengers
		ejected

Nonfiction Reading Practice, Grade 4 • EMC 3315 • ©2003 by Evan-Moor Corp.

Seat Belt Safety

What's Wrong with These Pictures?

What's Right About These Pictures?

The Unbuckled Seat Belt

It's after school. Kaitlyn is going home with her friend, Anna, to play. Anna's father waits in his car. Kaitlyn and Anna hop in the backseat.

"Buckle up, girls," Anna's father says, slipping on his seat belt.

Kaitlyn buckles her seat belt. But Anna doesn't. Anna's father starts up the car, and they zoom off.

Kaitlyn whispers to Anna, "Aren't you going to put on your seat belt?"

"No," Anna whispers back. "We're just going to my house."

Some people think they don't need to buckle up when they're riding around town. They aren't traveling far, and their car isn't going fast. But most deaths from car crashes happen close to home. And they usually happen when a car is going less than 40 miles per hour (64 km/h).

Kaitlyn glances at Anna's unbuckled seat belt. Then she looks out the window. Suddenly, a truck pulls out. "Watch out!"

Tires screech. "Hold on!" Anna's father shouts.

Kaitlyn's body slams against her seat belt. Anna screams and flies off the seat.

When a car stops suddenly, passengers tend to keep moving forward. Seat belts lock up and stop people from moving. But passengers who aren't wearing seat belts keep traveling.

Anna's face smacks the back of the seat. She drops to the car floor.

"We just missed the truck," Anna's father says. "Are you two OK?"

"I am," Kaitlyn replies.

"I'm not," Anna moans, climbing onto the seat. Her nose is bleeding. There's a gash on her forehead. "I wasn't wearing my seat belt."

Kaitlyn was sorry that her friend was injured. But she noticed that Anna always buckled up after that.

People who don't buckle up can be hurt. They sometimes suffer serious injuries. People can also die. About 40,000 people die in car crashes each year. Half of those people might still be alive if they had worn their seat belts.

Name _____

The Unbuckled Seat Belt

Fill in the bubble to answer each question or complete each sentence.

1. Most car crashes happen _____.
   - Ⓐ far out in the country
   - Ⓑ when someone is on a long trip
   - Ⓒ close to a person's own home
   - Ⓓ on the freeway

2. Why did Anna fly off the seat in the story?
   - Ⓐ Kaitlyn pushed her off the seat.
   - Ⓑ Anna wasn't wearing a seat belt.
   - Ⓒ Anna's father stopped too fast.
   - Ⓓ The tires screeched.

3. When a car stops suddenly, people inside it _____.
   - Ⓐ stop just as fast
   - Ⓑ should put on their seat belts right away
   - Ⓒ should drop to the floor
   - Ⓓ tend to keep moving forward inside the car

4. What can happen to people who don't wear their seat belts?
   - Ⓐ They can have serious injuries.
   - Ⓑ They usually escape injury.
   - Ⓒ Nothing ever happens to them.
   - Ⓓ They get upset with people who wear seat belts.

5. About _____ people die in car accidents each year.
   - Ⓐ   5
   - Ⓑ   1,000
   - Ⓒ   40,000
   - Ⓓ 1,000,000

Bonus: On the back of this page, explain why Anna always buckled up after she fell on the car floor that day.

Questions and Answers About Seat Belts

Why wear a seat belt?

When a car stops quickly, your body jerks forward. If the car stops fast enough, your body might fly off the seat. You may not stop until you hit the dashboard or windshield. You could even be thrown from the car. Seat belts hold you in your seat. They also keep you inside the car, which is the safest place to be.

How do seat belts work?

Most seat belts have two parts. The shoulder belt crosses over your collarbone. It keeps your upper body in place. The lap belt passes over your hipbones. It holds your lower body against the seat. You should wear both parts to be safe.

What are child safety seats?

Seat belts don't fit young children and babies. Shoulder belts don't properly cross their collarbones. Lap belts may not hold them in place. Child safety seats are made just for babies and young children.

Can parents hold children on their laps?

You might think children are easy to hold onto during a crash. But when a car stops suddenly, the child's body keeps moving forward. Someone holding the child no longer holds just the child's weight. He also has to keep her from flying out of his arms. This makes a child feel much heavier. A child can feel as if she weighs hundreds of pounds! Babies and young children should ride in child safety seats. Older children should wear seat belts.

Do I have to wear a seat belt if my car has air bags?

In a crash, air bags automatically pop out to cushion your body. But you must still wear a seat belt. It keeps you in the correct position so you hit the airbag at the right spot. Babies and children shouldn't sit in the front seat. Front air bags come out with great force and can cause harm.

Do I have to wear a seat belt around town?

Crashes most often happen close to a person's home. But they can happen anywhere. You should wear a seat belt whenever you're riding in a car.

Nonfiction Reading Practice, Grade 4 • EMC 3315 • ©2003 by Evan-Moor Corp.

Name _____

Questions and Answers About Seat Belts

Fill in the bubble to answer each question or complete each sentence.

1. A seat belt _____.
   - Ⓐ pushes people forward through the car
   - Ⓑ isn't always safe to wear
   - Ⓒ is good for babies to wear
   - Ⓓ holds people in their seat

2. What are a shoulder belt and a lap belt?
   - Ⓐ two parts of a car
   - Ⓑ two parts of an airbag
   - Ⓒ two parts of a seat belt
   - Ⓓ two parts of a child safety seat

3. Why should people not hold babies on their laps?
   - Ⓐ The baby might cry.
   - Ⓑ A baby is too difficult to hold onto in a crash.
   - Ⓒ The seat belt might crush the baby.
   - Ⓓ Babies don't like to be held in cars.

4. Why should people wear seat belts if their car has air bags?
   - Ⓐ The seat belt won't hold people in place unless there are air bags.
   - Ⓑ The air bag won't pop out unless the person is wearing a seat belt.
   - Ⓒ The seat belt keeps the person in the correct position.
   - Ⓓ People do not have to wear a seat belt when there are air bags.

5. Crashes happen _____.
   - Ⓐ anywhere
   - Ⓑ only near a person's home
   - Ⓒ only when a car is traveling slowly
   - Ⓓ only on the freeway

Bonus: Pretend you see someone riding in a car who is not wearing a seat belt. On the back of this page, write two things you would say to that person to convince him or her to wear a seat belt.

Seat Belt Physics

Someone is traveling in a car. A truck pulls out in front of the car, and the car slams into the truck. What happens to the car? What happens to the person inside it?

Physics can help answer these questions. Physics is a field of science that deals with matter and energy. Matter is anything that takes up space. Water and bells are matter because they take up space. So are cars and people. Energy is an activity that changes matter. Heat energy causes water to become warm, and sound energy allows people to hear bells. Movement energy makes cars and people move.

Physicists have studied matter and energy and have formulated rules to help explain them. One of these rules is the Law of Inertia. It states that once an object is moving, it keeps moving. The object stops only when something forces it to stop.

The Law of Inertia applies to automobiles. Once a car is moving, the motor keeps it moving. It stops only when something forces it to stop. Usually, brakes do. But when a car hits a truck, the truck forces it to stop.

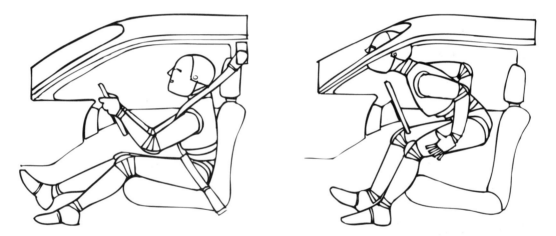

The Law of Inertia also applies to passengers. Before the crash, the passenger moves down the road because the car carries her along. During the crash, the car stops, but the passenger doesn't. That's because the passenger herself didn't hit the truck. The passenger, therefore, continues moving forward inside the stopped car. She moves at the speed the car was going when it hit the truck.

The passenger keeps moving until something forces her to stop. Sometimes, she is stopped by the dashboard or windshield, which can cause her great injury. She might even be ejected from the car. Most people thrown from a car die.

But what should have forced the passenger to stop in the first place was her seat belt! Seat belts help hold passengers in their seats.

Our country has laws saying people must wear seat belts. Not everyone obeys these laws. But passengers always obey the Law of Inertia.

Name _____

Seat Belt Physics

Fill in the bubble to answer each question.

1. What is *physics*?
   - Ⓐ It's a field of science that deals with matter and energy.
   - Ⓑ It's what something looks like.
   - Ⓒ It's an object that changes matter into energy.
   - Ⓓ It's a type of energy used in science experiments.

2. What is the Law of Inertia?
   - Ⓐ People must wear seat belts at all times.
   - Ⓑ Drive slowly with passengers inside the car.
   - Ⓒ Once an object is moving, it keeps moving until it runs out of energy.
   - Ⓓ Once an object is moving, it keeps moving until something forces it to stop.

3. How does the Law of Inertia apply to automobiles?
   - Ⓐ Once a car is moving, it is hard to stop it.
   - Ⓑ Once a car is in motion, there is nothing that can stop it from crashing.
   - Ⓒ Once a car is moving, the motor keeps it moving until you put on the brakes.
   - Ⓓ Once a car is moving slowly, there is no need for seat belts.

4. If a car stops suddenly, what do passengers inside tend to do?
   - Ⓐ They stop suddenly.
   - Ⓑ They keep moving at the speed the car had been going.
   - Ⓒ They turn into matter.
   - Ⓓ They keep moving faster and faster through the car.

5. What will most likely happen to a passenger if she is ejected from the car?
   - Ⓐ She will be injured.
   - Ⓑ She will hit the dashboard.
   - Ⓒ She will hear bells.
   - Ⓓ She will die.

Bonus: On the back of this page, explain what this saying means: "Passengers always obey the Law of Inertia."

Dr. Charles Richard Drew

Introducing the Topic

1. Reproduce page 103 for individual students, or make a transparency to use with a group or the whole class.

2. Tell students that all day long their hearts pump blood throughout their bodies. Explain that without blood, people can die. That's why there are special places called blood banks. They store blood in case people need it in emergencies or during operations. Show students the blood bank pictures.

Reading the Selections

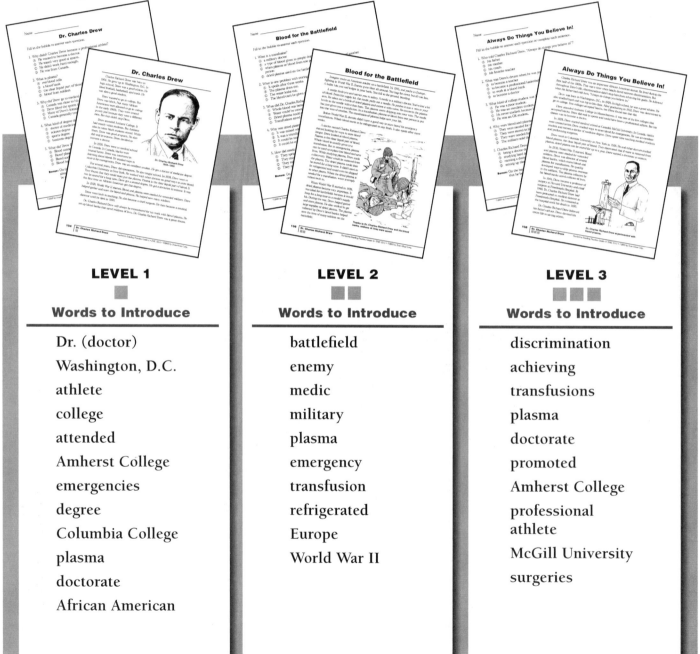

LEVEL 1
■

Words to Introduce

Dr. (doctor)
Washington, D.C.
athlete
college
attended
Amherst College
emergencies
degree
Columbia College
plasma
doctorate
African American

LEVEL 2
■ ■

Words to Introduce

battlefield
enemy
medic
military
plasma
emergency
transfusion
refrigerated
Europe
World War II

LEVEL 3
■ ■ ■

Words to Introduce

discrimination
achieving
transfusions
plasma
doctorate
promoted
Amherst College
professional
athlete
McGill University
surgeries

Nonfiction Reading Practice, Grade 4 • EMC 3315 • ©2003 by Evan-Moor Corp.

Blood Banks

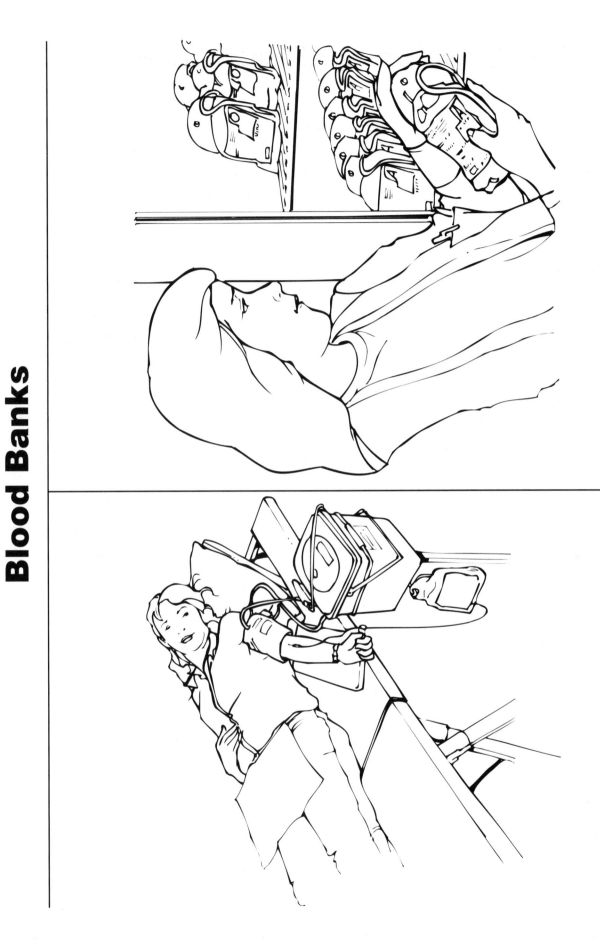

This woman is doing a good deed by donating much-needed blood.

Blood banks store the woman's blood in case people need it in emergencies or during operations.

Dr. Charles Drew

Charles Richard Drew was born in 1904. He grew up in Washington, D.C. In high school, Drew was a good athlete. He liked football, basketball, and track. He was also a good student.

Drew wanted to go to college. But Drew was black. Not many African Americans were allowed to go to college in the early 1900s. They were treated poorly just because they were a different race. But that didn't stop Drew.

Drew attended Amherst College. It had mostly white students. But Amherst also let some black students attend. While there, Drew was good at sports. He also did well in science. Drew decided to become a doctor.

In 1928, Drew went to medical school in Canada. In Canada, blacks were treated better. Drew was interested in learning about blood. He studied ways to

**Dr. Charles Richard Drew
1904–1950**

store it for emergencies. Drew was an excellent student. He got a doctor of medicine degree.

For several years, Drew did operations. He also taught school. In 1938, Drew went to Columbia University in New York. He worked with other doctors on good ways to store blood. They found that they could store just the plasma. Plasma is the clear liquid part of blood. It can be stored for a long time. Drew got a second degree. He got a doctorate in science. It was the first time an African American got this degree.

In 1939, World War II started. Blood and plasma were needed for wounded soldiers. Drew helped gather and store the blood and plasma. He helped save many soldiers.

Drew went back to teaching. He also became a chief surgeon. He then became a medical director until he died in 1950.

Dr. Charles Richard Drew will always be remembered for his work with blood plasma. He set up blood banks that saved millions of lives. Dr. Charles Richard Drew was a great doctor.

Nonfiction Reading Practice, Grade 4 • EMC 3315 • ©2003 by Evan-Moor Corp.

Name _____

Dr. Charles Drew

Fill in the bubble to answer each question.

1. Why didn't Charles Drew become a professional athlete?
   - Ⓐ He wanted to become a doctor.
   - Ⓑ He wasn't very good at sports.
   - Ⓒ He didn't work hard enough.
   - Ⓓ He was from Canada.

2. What is *plasma*?
   - Ⓐ red blood cells
   - Ⓑ a blood bank
   - Ⓒ the clear liquid part of blood
   - Ⓓ blood from soldiers

3. Why did Drew go to medical school in Canada?
   - Ⓐ Canada was close to his home.
   - Ⓑ Drew liked the sports in Canada.
   - Ⓒ Many of Drew's friends went to college there.
   - Ⓓ Canada generally treated blacks well.

4. What kind of degree did Drew get in Canada?
   - Ⓐ doctor of medicine
   - Ⓑ science degree
   - Ⓒ sports degree
   - Ⓓ business degree

5. What did Drew find out about storing blood?
   - Ⓐ Blood cannot be stored.
   - Ⓑ Blood plasma can be stored for a long time.
   - Ⓒ Blood and plasma cannot be stored together.
   - Ⓓ Blood has to be stored all together.

Bonus: On the back of this page, write why Dr. Charles Richard Drew will
always be remembered.

Blood for the Battlefield

Imagine you're an American soldier on a battlefield. It's 1945, and you're in Europe, fighting in World War II. Enemy guns blast all around. You leap for cover, but it's too late. A bullet hits you and lodges in your back. You fall to the ground, bleeding.

A medic finds you and carries you to safety. A medic is a military doctor. You've lost a lot of blood. From his supply kit, the medic pulls out a needle. He pushes it into a vein in your arm. He takes out a bottle of dried plasma and mixes it with water. He connects the plasma bottle to the needle with a thin hose. The plasma starts dripping into your vein. The medic has just given you a transfusion. In a transfusion, plasma or blood from one person is put into the vein of another. The transfusion of plasma helps save your life.

Before World War II, doctors didn't have a good way to store blood for emergency transfusions. Whole blood needs to be refrigerated to stay fresh. It also spoils after three weeks.

A doctor named Charles Richard Drew started looking for ways to store blood longer. Drew looked at blood plasma. Plasma is the clear liquid part of blood. Whole blood is usually given in a transfusion. But in emergencies, plasma can be used to replace lost blood and save lives. While studying plasma, Drew made a discovery. Water could be removed from the plasma. The dried plasma could then be stored for a long time. It didn't need to be refrigerated and could even be shipped to other places. When the dried plasma is needed for a transfusion, water is simply mixed back in.

When World War II started in 1939, dried plasma became very important. It was ideal for battlefields because it would keep for a long time in a medic's supply kit. During the war, Drew helped gather and store plasma. He also worked to get large supplies of dried plasma. The plasma collected by Drew's blood banks helped save the lives of many soldiers on the battlefield.

Thanks to Dr. Charles Richard Drew and his blood banks, millions of lives were saved.

Nonfiction Reading Practice, Grade 4 • EMC 3315 • ©2003 by Evan-Moor Corp.

Name _____

Blood for the Battlefield

Fill in the bubble to answer each question.

1. What is a *transfusion*?
   - Ⓐ a military doctor
   - Ⓑ a type of blood given to people during wars
   - Ⓒ when plasma or blood from one person is put into the vein of another person
   - Ⓓ dried plasma used on the battlefield

2. What is one problem with storing whole blood?
   - Ⓐ It spoils after three weeks.
   - Ⓑ The plasma dries out.
   - Ⓒ The water leaks out.
   - Ⓓ The blood can't be given to people.

3. What did Dr. Charles Richard Drew discover?
   - Ⓐ Whole blood was better than dried blood.
   - Ⓑ Water could be removed from plasma.
   - Ⓒ Dried plasma could spoil in three weeks.
   - Ⓓ Transfusions saved lives.

4. Why was dried plasma important during World War II?
   - Ⓐ It was mixed with water to make it liquid.
   - Ⓑ It was a transfusion.
   - Ⓒ It could be stored for a long time without spoiling.
   - Ⓓ It could be collected by the soldiers.

5. How did medics use dried plasma on the battlefield?
   - Ⓐ They sprinkled the dried plasma on wounds.
   - Ⓑ They mixed it with other shipments of plasma.
   - Ⓒ They mixed it with stored blood and water.
   - Ⓓ They mixed it with water.

Bonus: On the back of this page, explain what might have happened to soldiers on the battlefield if medics didn't have dried plasma.

Always Do Things You Believe In!

Charles Richard Drew was an important African American doctor. He lived during the first half of the 1900s. This was a time when blacks faced extreme discrimination. But throughout Drew's life, discrimination didn't stop him from achieving his goals. He followed what his father had told him, "Always do things you believe in."

Drew was born in Washington, D.C., in 1904. In high school, he was a good athlete. He also studied hard and was top in his class. After graduating in 1922, Drew was determined to go to college. Few colleges accepted blacks, but Drew found one that did.

Drew attended Amherst College in Massachusetts. It was one of the few colleges that accepted blacks. Drew did well in sports and could have been a professional athlete. But his dream was to become a doctor.

In 1928, Drew started medical school at Canada's McGill University. In Canada, blacks were treated better. Drew studied ways to store blood for emergencies. He was an excellent student and earned a doctor of medicine degree. Drew spent time teaching medical students and performing surgeries.

Drew went to Columbia University in New York in 1938. He and other doctors studied blood plasma, the clear liquid part of blood. They discovered that if water is removed from plasma, dried plasma can be stored for up to a year. Drew earned a doctorate in science.

In 1939, World War II started. Blood and plasma were needed for wounded soldiers. Drew was director of several blood banks, which stored blood and plasma for transfusions. He quickly developed ways to ship plasma overseas to the soldiers. The plasma collected by his blood banks saved millions of lives.

In 1941, Drew became a professor of surgery at Howard University and chief surgeon at Freedman's Hospital. By 1946, Dr. Charles Richard Drew had been promoted to medical director at Freedman's Hospital. He remained at the hospital until his death in 1950.

Dr. Charles Richard Drew followed his father's advice. Drew devoted his entire life to saving others.

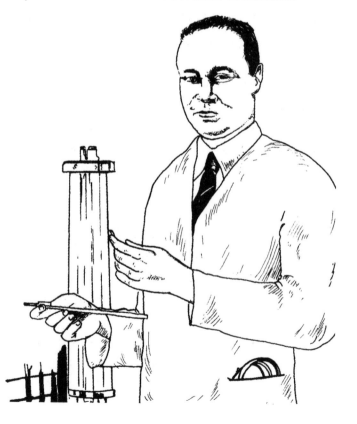

Dr. Charles Richard Drew experimented with blood plasma.

Nonfiction Reading Practice, Grade 4 • EMC 3315 • ©2003 by Evan-Moor Corp.

Name _____

Always Do Things You Believe In!

Fill in the bubble to answer each question or complete each sentence.

1. Who told Charles Richard Drew, "Always do things you believe in"?
   - Ⓐ his father
   - Ⓑ his mother
   - Ⓒ his coach
   - Ⓓ his favorite teacher

2. What was Drew's dream when he was young?
   - Ⓐ to become a teacher
   - Ⓑ to become a professional basketball player
   - Ⓒ to work at a blood bank
   - Ⓓ to become a doctor

3. What kind of college student was Drew?
   - Ⓐ He was a poor student.
   - Ⓑ He was an excellent student.
   - Ⓒ He never studied, because he was playing sports.
   - Ⓓ He was an OK student.

4. Why were blood and plasma important during the war?
   - Ⓐ They were needed for new types of operations.
   - Ⓑ They were stored in blood banks.
   - Ⓒ They were needed for wounded soldiers.
   - Ⓓ The military sold them to make money.

5. Charles Richard Drew is best remembered for _____.
   - Ⓐ being a doctor during the war
   - Ⓑ studying hard in school
   - Ⓒ earning a doctor of mathematics degree
   - Ⓓ setting up blood banks and working with blood plasma

Bonus: On the back of this page, describe two things Charles Richard Drew did that he believed in.

Structural Engineers

Introducing the Topic

1. Reproduce page 111 for individual students, or make a transparency to use with a group or the whole class.

2. Ask students if they've ever looked up at a tall building. Have they ever wondered what makes the building stand up? Show students the picture. Point out the building parts that help hold it up.

Reading the Selections

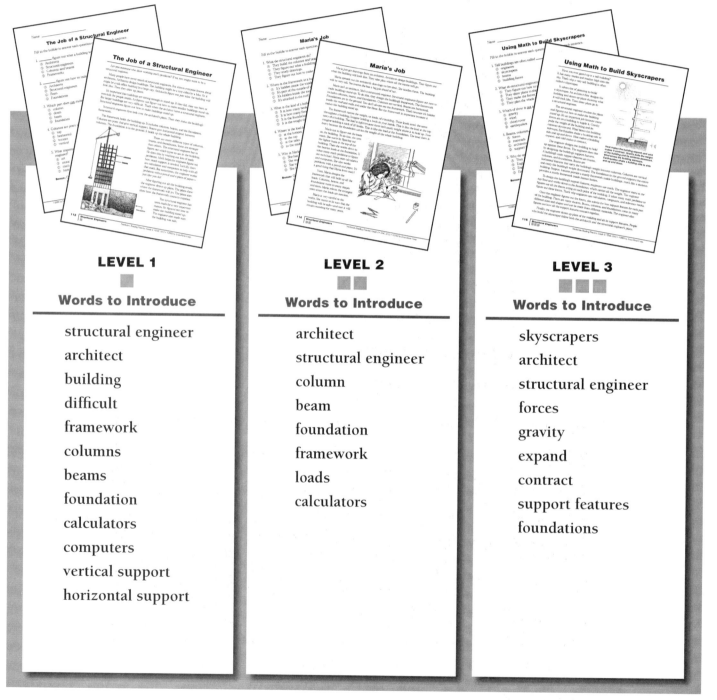

LEVEL 1

Words to Introduce

structural engineer
architect
building
difficult
framework
columns
beams
foundation
calculators
computers
vertical support
horizontal support

LEVEL 2

Words to Introduce

architect
structural engineer
column
beam
foundation
framework
loads
calculators

LEVEL 3

Words to Introduce

skyscrapers
architect
structural engineer
forces
gravity
expand
contract
support features
foundations

Nonfiction Reading Practice, Grade 4 • EMC 3315 • ©2003 by Evan-Moor Corp.

Building a Skyscraper

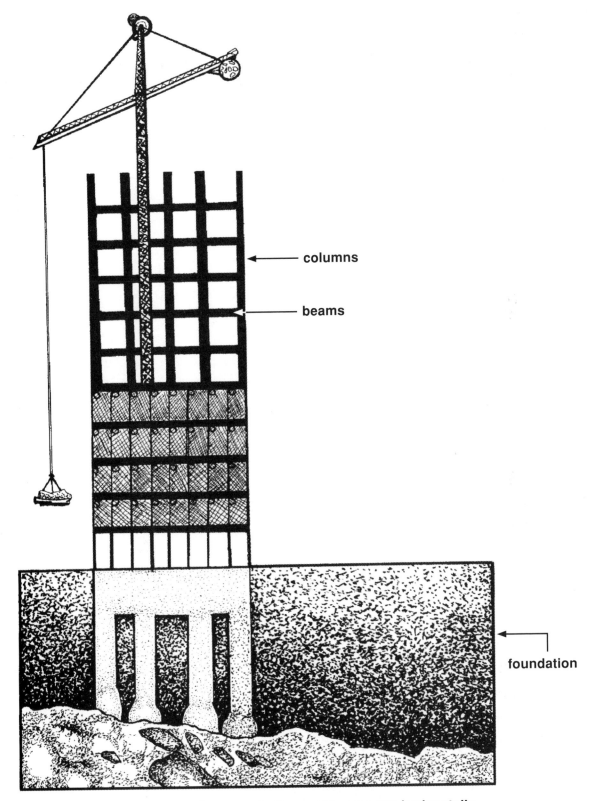

columns

beams

foundation

Skyscrapers need a strong framework. Support beams run horizontally. Columns are heavy vertical supports. The foundation is the main support system for the building.

The Job of a Structural Engineer

Are you someone who likes working math problems? If so, you might want to be a structural engineer.

Many people have never heard of structural engineers. But almost everyone knows about architects. Architects design buildings. The building might be a tiny cabin by a lake. Or it might be a tall office building in a large city. Architects figure out just what the building will look like. Then they draw up plans.

It's important that buildings are strong enough to stand up. If they fall, they can hurt or even kill the people inside. Architects can figure out how to make smaller buildings stand up. But larger buildings are very difficult. That's when the architect hires a structural engineer. Structural engineers figure out how to make buildings stand up.

Structural engineers first look over the architect's plans. Then they make the building's framework.

The framework holds the building up. It includes columns, beams, and the foundation. Columns are posts that give vertical support. Beams give horizontal support between columns. The foundation is in the ground. It holds up the whole building.

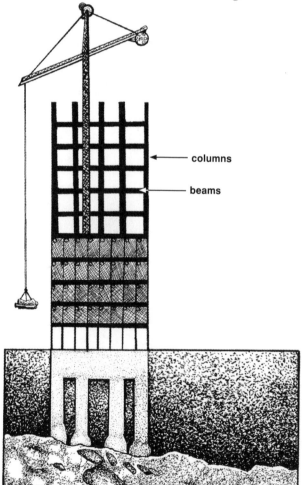

columns

beams

foundation

There are many different types of columns, beams, and foundations. Some are stronger than others. The structural engineer has to figure out which types to use in the building. He does this by working out lots of math problems. Math helps the engineer figure out how much support is needed. Luckily, there are calculators and computers to help with all that math. But sometimes, the engineer works problems with a pencil and a piece of paper—just like you do!

After figuring out all the building needs, the engineer draws up plans. The plans show where the framework will go. The plans also show how the framework connects together.

The structural engineer has used math for a very important reason. He figured out how to make the building stand up. The engineer also made sure the building was safe.

Name _____

The Job of a Structural Engineer

Fill in the bubble to answer each question or complete each sentence.

1. _____ figure out what a building will look like.
   - Ⓐ Architects
   - Ⓑ Structural engineers
   - Ⓒ Columns and beams
   - Ⓓ Frameworks

2. _____ figure out how to make tall buildings stand up.
   - Ⓐ Architects
   - Ⓑ Structural engineers
   - Ⓒ Posts
   - Ⓓ Foundations

3. Which part does <u>not</u> make up the framework?
   - Ⓐ column
   - Ⓑ doors
   - Ⓒ beam
   - Ⓓ foundation

4. Columns are posts that give _____ support.
   - Ⓐ top
   - Ⓑ horizontal
   - Ⓒ bottom
   - Ⓓ vertical

5. What important subject should a person study to become a structural engineer?
   - Ⓐ art
   - Ⓑ music
   - Ⓒ math
   - Ⓓ history

Bonus: On the back of this page, draw and label a picture of a column and a beam.

Maria's Job

Maria just got drawings from an architect. Architects design buildings. They figure out what the building will look like. They also plan where all the rooms will go.

Maria spreads out the architect's drawings on her desk. She studies them. The building will be very tall. She knows she has a big job ahead of her.

Maria isn't an architect. She's a structural engineer. Structural engineers figure out how to make buildings stand up. To do this, they design the building's framework. The framework includes columns, beams, and foundations. Columns are vertical. Beams are horizontal. Foundations are in the ground. You don't always see the framework. That's because it's hidden inside the roof and walls and under the floor. But the framework is important because it makes the building stand up.

The framework carries the weight, or loads, of a building. These loads aren't the same throughout a building. Imagine holding a book in your hands. This is like the load at the top story of a building. The load is light because there isn't much weight above it to hold up. Now imagine holding a stack of 10 books. This is like the load at the foundation. The load there is heavy because the foundation carries the weight of the whole building.

Maria has to figure out the loads on the building. To do this, she uses math. She starts by figuring out the lighter loads at the top of the building. Then she works down to the heavier loads at the foundation. It takes many math problems to figure out each load. Maria uses calculators and computers. She also works problems with a pencil and paper. It's a good thing that Maria loves math!

Next, Maria designs the framework that will hold up all the loads. Columns, beams, and foundations come in many shapes and sizes. Maria selects the strongest ones where the loads are heaviest.

Maria is very careful as she works. She wants to be sure that the building will be safe—and that it will remain standing for many years.

Name _____

Maria's Job

Fill in the bubble to answer each question.

1. What do structural engineers do?
   - Ⓐ They build the columns and beams.
   - Ⓑ They figure out what a building will look like.
   - Ⓒ They study drawings.
   - Ⓓ They figure out how to make a building stand up.

2. Where is the framework in a building?
   - Ⓐ It's hidden inside the windows and doors.
   - Ⓑ It's part of the outside of the building.
   - Ⓒ It's hidden inside the roof, walls, and under the floor.
   - Ⓓ It's attached to the roof to hold it up.

3. What is the *load* of a building?
   - Ⓐ It is how many books there are in the building.
   - Ⓑ It is how many floors there are in the building.
   - Ⓒ It is the foundation below the building.
   - Ⓓ It is the weight the building carries.

4. Where is the load heaviest in a building?
   - Ⓐ at the bottom
   - Ⓑ at the top
   - Ⓒ at the sides
   - Ⓓ in the middle

5. Why is Maria careful when she works?
   - Ⓐ She has a lot of math to do.
   - Ⓑ She wants to be sure the building is safe.
   - Ⓒ She wants to please the architect.
   - Ⓓ She has to make all the loads.

Bonus: On the back of this page, explain why it's a good thing that Maria loves math.

Using Math to Build Skyscrapers

Have you ever gazed up at a tall building? It has many stories and reaches high into the sky. That's why a very tall building is often called a skyscraper.

It takes a lot of planning to build a skyscraper. An architect first designs the building and draws up plans showing what it will look like. Then these plans go to a structural engineer.

The structural engineer studies the plans and figures out how to make the building stand up. It's an important job because many forces act on a building to topple it. Gravity pulls the weight of the building and its contents downward. Wind blows the building sideways. Earthquakes shake a building side to side and up and down. Heat makes a building expand, and cold makes it contract.

The engineer designs the building to hold up against these forces. The engineer does this by designing the building's support features. A building's main support features are beams, columns, and foundations. Beams are horizontal features that carry the building's weight between columns. Columns are vertical and carry the building's weight downward. The foundation in the ground supports the entire building. Support features provide a sturdy framework inside buildings, much like a skeleton provides a sturdy framework inside human bodies.

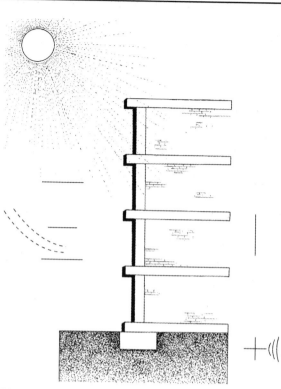

Heat makes the building expand, and cold makes it contract. Gravity pulls the weight of the building and its contents downward. Wind blows the building sideways. Earthquakes shake a building side to side and up and down.

To design the building's support features, engineers use math. The engineer starts at the top floor and works down to the foundation, which carries all the weight. The engineer figures out all the forces acting on each point of the building. It takes many math problems to figure out these forces. That's why engineers use calculators, computers, and reference books.

Once the engineer figures out the forces, she selects the best support feature for each part of the building. There are many choices. Beams, columns, and foundations come in many different sizes and shapes and can be made from different materials. The engineer also figures out how all the support features connect together.

Finally, the engineer draws up plans of the building and all its support features. People who build the skyscraper follow both the architect's and the structural engineer's plans.

Nonfiction Reading Practice, Grade 4 • EMC 3315 • ©2003 by Evan-Moor Corp.

Name _____

Using Math to Build Skyscrapers

Fill in the bubble to answer each question or complete each sentence.

1. Tall buildings are often called _____.
   - Ⓐ engineers
   - Ⓑ skyscrapers
   - Ⓒ beams
   - Ⓓ building forces

2. What do structural engineers do?
   - Ⓐ They figure out how to make a building stand up.
   - Ⓑ They draw plans to show what a building will look like.
   - Ⓒ They make the forces in a building.
   - Ⓓ They plan the whole building.

3. Which of these is <u>not</u> a force that acts on a building?
   - Ⓐ gravity
   - Ⓑ wind
   - Ⓒ cloud cover
   - Ⓓ earthquakes

4. Beams, columns, and the foundation are a building's main _____.
   - Ⓐ forces
   - Ⓑ materials
   - Ⓒ architects
   - Ⓓ support features

5. Why do engineers use calculators, computers, and reference books?
   - Ⓐ They help the engineer figure out all the math problems.
   - Ⓑ Engineers aren't good at math.
   - Ⓒ Engineers use them to make the architectural plans.
   - Ⓓ Engineers use them to find gravity under the building.

Bonus: On the back of this page, explain why it's important that a structural engineer carefully design a building so it will stand up.

Probability

Introducing the Topic

1. Reproduce page 119 for individual students or for groups of students.

2. Provide each student or group of students with a single die. Have students follow the directions on the probability worksheet. After they are finished, discuss the results. Tell students they are going to learn more about probability as they read the articles in the unit.

Reading the Selections

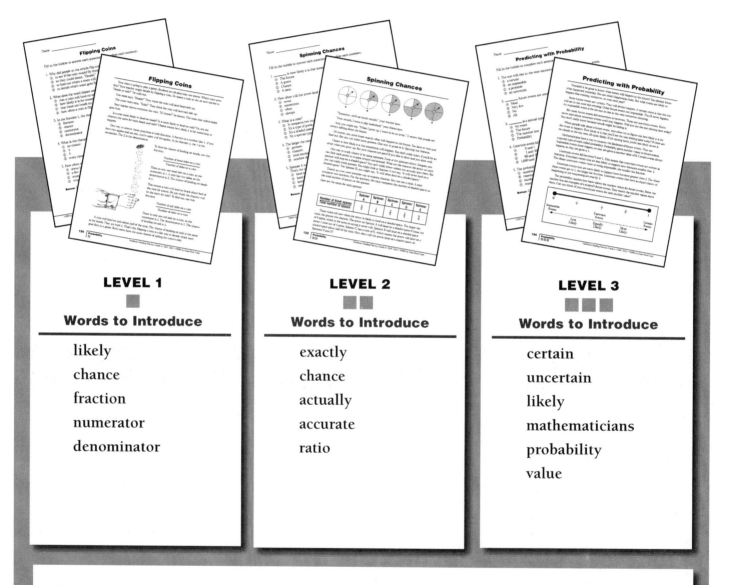

LEVEL 1
■

Words to Introduce

likely

chance

fraction

numerator

denominator

LEVEL 2
■ ■

Words to Introduce

exactly

chance

actually

accurate

ratio

LEVEL 3
■ ■ ■

Words to Introduce

certain

uncertain

likely

mathematicians

probability

value

Part One answers: 1. one-in-six chance (1/6)   2. one-in-six chance (1/6)   3. three-in-six chance, or one-half of the time (3/6 or 1/2)   4. three-in-six chance, or one-half of the time (3/6 or 1/2)

Part Two answers: Answers on the tally sheet will vary. But during discussion, help students to realize that, no matter how many times the die is rolled, the probability of rolling each number remains a one-in-six chance.

Nonfiction Reading Practice, Grade 4 • EMC 3315 • ©2003 by Evan-Moor Corp.

Name _____

Probability Using a Die

Part One

Look at a single die. Without rolling the die, answer the following questions.

1. What is the chance you will roll the number *1*?

    _____

2. What is the chance you will roll the number *6*?

    _____

3. What is the chance you will roll an *even* number?

    _____

4. What is the chance you will roll an *odd* number?

    _____

Part Two

Use this tally sheet to record the number on the die each time you roll it. Roll the die 10 times in a row.

Tally Sheet

Number Rolled	Number of Rolls
Number 1 ⚀	
Number 2 ⚁	
Number 3 ⚂	
Number 4 ⚃	
Number 5 ⚄	
Number 6 ⚅	

Compare the results with the class. Discuss why the results turned out the way they did.

Flipping Coins

Your class is going to play a game. Students are divided into two teams. Which team goes first? Your teacher might decide by flipping a coin. He tosses a coin in the air and catches it. "Heads or tails?" he calls out.

One team says, "Heads!" They think the coin will land head side up.

The other team says, "Tails!" They think the coin will land tail side up.

Your teacher shows everyone the coin. "It's heads!" he shouts. The team that called heads goes first.

Is a coin more likely to land on heads? Is it more likely to land on tails? Or, are the chances the same for both heads and tails? *Chance* means how likely it is for something to happen.

One way to answer these questions is with fractions. A fraction is a number like $\frac{1}{2}$. If you have two apples and eat one, you've eaten $\frac{1}{2}$ of the apples. In the fraction $\frac{1}{2}$, the 1 is the numerator. The 2 is the denominator.

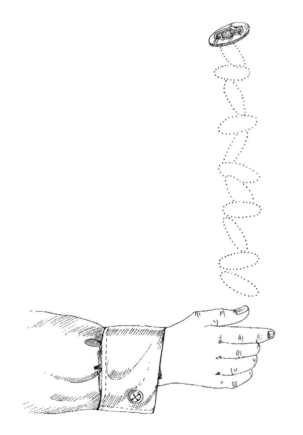

To find the chance of landing on heads, use this fraction:

$$\frac{\text{Number of head sides on a coin}}{\text{Number of sides on a coin}}$$

There is only one head side on a coin, so the numerator is 1. A coin has two sides, so the denominator is 2. The chance of landing on heads is $\frac{1}{2}$.

This means a coin will land on heads about half of the time it's tossed. Do you think the chances will be the same for tails? To find out, use this fraction:

$$\frac{\text{Number of tail sides on a coin}}{\text{Number of sides on a coin}}$$

There is only one tail side on a coin, so the numerator is 1. The denominator is 2. The chance of landing on tails is $\frac{1}{2}$.

A coin will land on tails about half of the time. The chance of landing on tails is the same as for heads. They are both $\frac{1}{2}$. That's why flipping a coin is a fair way to decide which team goes first in a game. Both teams have the same chance of calling the correct side.

Nonfiction Reading Practice, Grade 4 • EMC 3315 • ©2003 by Evan-Moor Corp.

Name _____

Flipping Coins

Fill in the bubble to answer each question or complete each sentence.

1. Why did people in the article flip coins?
   - Ⓐ to see if the coin would fly through the air
   - Ⓑ so they could shout, "Heads!"
   - Ⓒ to find out where a team will play in the field
   - Ⓓ to decide which team goes first in a game

2. What does the word *chance* mean?
   - Ⓐ that a coin will land on something
   - Ⓑ how likely it is for something to happen
   - Ⓒ that there are heads on a coin
   - Ⓓ how often a coin is flipped in the air

3. In the fraction $\frac{1}{2}$, the number 1 is the _____.
   - Ⓐ fraction
   - Ⓑ chance
   - Ⓒ numerator
   - Ⓓ denominator

4. What is the chance of landing on heads when a coin is tossed?
   - Ⓐ no chance
   - Ⓑ $\frac{1}{2}$
   - Ⓒ $\frac{2}{1}$
   - Ⓓ every time

5. How often will a coin land on tails?
   - Ⓐ about half of the time
   - Ⓑ a few times
   - Ⓒ most of the time
   - Ⓓ whenever it's tossed

Bonus: On the back of this page, explain why flipping a coin is a fair way to decide which team goes first in a game.

Spinning Chances

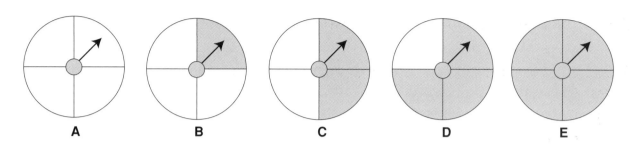

A   B   C   D   E

"Tomorrow, we'll eat lunch outside," your teacher says.

"Next month, I want to play basketball," your friend says.

And, you might say, "When I grow up, I want to be an artist." It seems that people are always talking about the future.

Of course, you never know exactly what will happen in the future. You have to wait and find out. But you can make some guesses. One way to guess is by figuring out chances.

Chance is how likely it is that something will happen. You don't really know if you'll be an artist when you grow up. But your chances are good if you like to draw and you draw well.

One way to study chance is by using spinners. Look at the spinners above. Imagine you can flick each arrow so it spins around and around. What are the chances the arrow on each spinner will stop on a shaded space? You can't really know unless you actually spin them. But you can make some guesses. You might look at Spinner A and say, "It will never land on a shaded space." For Spinner D, you might say, "It will often land on a shaded space."

There's an even more accurate way to express chances. You can use a ratio. A ratio compares two numbers. For the spinners, the ratio compares the number of shaded spaces to the total number of spaces on the spinner. Here are the ratios for each spinner:

	Spinner A	Spinner B	Spinner C	Spinner D	Spinner E
Number of shaded spaces / **Total number of spaces**	$\frac{0}{4}$	$\frac{1}{4}$	$\frac{2}{4}$	$\frac{3}{4}$	$\frac{4}{4}$

These ratios tell how often the arrow is likely to land on a shaded space. The larger the ratio, the greater the chances. The arrow on Spinner A will land on a shaded space 0 times out of 4 spins, which is the same as saying it never will. Spinner B will land on a shaded space about 1 time out of 4 spins. Spinner C has a ratio of $\frac{2}{4}$, which means the arrow will land on a shaded space about half of the time. How often will the arrow land on a shaded space on Spinners D and E?

Nonfiction Reading Practice, Grade 4 • EMC 3315 • ©2003 by Evan-Moor Corp.

Name _____

Spinning Chances

Fill in the bubble to answer each question or complete each sentence.

1. _____ is how likely it is that something will happen.
   - Ⓐ The future
   - Ⓑ A guess
   - Ⓒ Chance
   - Ⓓ A ratio

2. How often will the arrow land on a shaded space on Spinner E?
   - Ⓐ never
   - Ⓑ sometimes
   - Ⓒ often
   - Ⓓ always

3. What is a *ratio*?
   - Ⓐ It compares two numbers.
   - Ⓑ It's a type of guess.
   - Ⓒ It's a shaded space on a spinner.
   - Ⓓ It's a special type of spinner.

4. The larger the ratio, the greater the _____.
   - Ⓐ guesses
   - Ⓑ chances
   - Ⓒ total number of spaces
   - Ⓓ number of times the arrow will spin around

5. Spinner A with no shaded spaces will land on a shaded space $\frac{0}{4}$ times. That's the same as saying the arrow will _____.
   - Ⓐ land on a shaded space half the time
   - Ⓑ land on a shaded space 4 times
   - Ⓒ land on a shaded space all the time
   - Ⓓ never land on a shaded space

Bonus: Say you are playing a spinning game with the spinners. Every time you spin the arrow and it lands on a shaded space on the spinner, you win. On the back of this page, explain which spinner—A, B, C, D, or E—gives you the greatest chance of winning the spinning game. Which spinner gives you the least chance?

Predicting with Probability

Wouldn't it be great to know what events will happen in the future? You already know what happened yesterday. You see what's happening today. But what events are likely to happen this evening, tomorrow, or even next year?

Some future events are certain. They will always happen. A certain event is that the sun will set in the west this evening. Other future events are impossible. They'll never happen. An impossible event is for the sun to rise in the west tomorrow morning.

But most future events fall somewhere in between. These are uncertain events. You're never sure about uncertain events until they happen. Will you see the sun shining later today? You don't really know because clouds might be hiding it.

When people talk about a future event, they often try to figure out how likely it is for the event to happen. How likely is it that you'll see the sun shining later today? If there are no clouds in the sky now, it's quite likely. If it's raining hard, you're less likely to see it.

Mathematicians have a way to measure the likeliness of future events. They use a special type of math called probability. Probability gives number values to future events. Impossible events never happen, so they are given a number value of 0. Certain events always happen, so they are given a 1.

Uncertain events fall between 0 and 1. This means that uncertain events are written as fractions. Uncertain events that are less likely to happen have fractions smaller than $\frac{1}{2}$. The closer uncertain events come to being impossible, the smaller the fraction.

Uncertain events that are more likely to happen have fractions greater than $\frac{1}{2}$. The closer these events get to 1, the larger the fraction. Uncertain events that have an equal chance of happening or not happening are exactly $\frac{1}{2}$.

The probability number line below shows the number values for future events. Below the number line are examples of a student's future events. They match the number values above them. Can you think of your own future events for each number value?

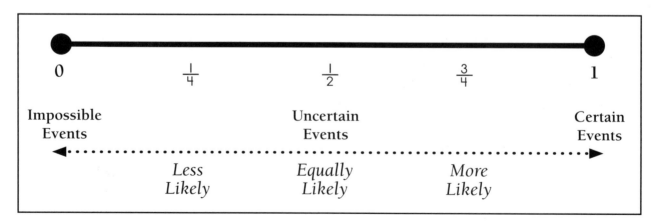

Name _____

Predicting with Probability

Fill in the bubble to complete each sentence.

1. The sun will rise in the west tomorrow morning. This is _____ event.
   - Ⓐ a certain
   - Ⓑ an impossible
   - Ⓒ a probable
   - Ⓓ an uncertain

2. _____ future events are uncertain.
   - Ⓐ Most
   - Ⓑ Very few
   - Ⓒ No
   - Ⓓ All

3. _____ is a special type of math.
   - Ⓐ An event
   - Ⓑ The future
   - Ⓒ The number line
   - Ⓓ Probability

4. *Uncertain events* fall between _____ on the probability number line.
   - Ⓐ   0 and 1
   - Ⓑ   1 and 100
   - Ⓒ   90 and 100
   - Ⓓ 1,000 and 10,000

5. The probability number line shows the _____.
   - Ⓐ number values of current events
   - Ⓑ reasons why events happen in the future
   - Ⓒ number values of future events
   - Ⓓ reasons why things probably happened in the past

Bonus: On the back of this page, draw the probability number line. Below each
number on the number line, write five of your own future events.

Owning a Business

Introducing the Topic

1. Reproduce page 127 for individual students, or make a transparency to use with a group or the whole class.

2. Show the pictures of different kinds of small businesses. Ask students if they know anyone who owns a business. What kind? What kind of business would the students like to own one day? Tell them they will be reading about types of businesses anyone—including children—can own.

Reading the Selections

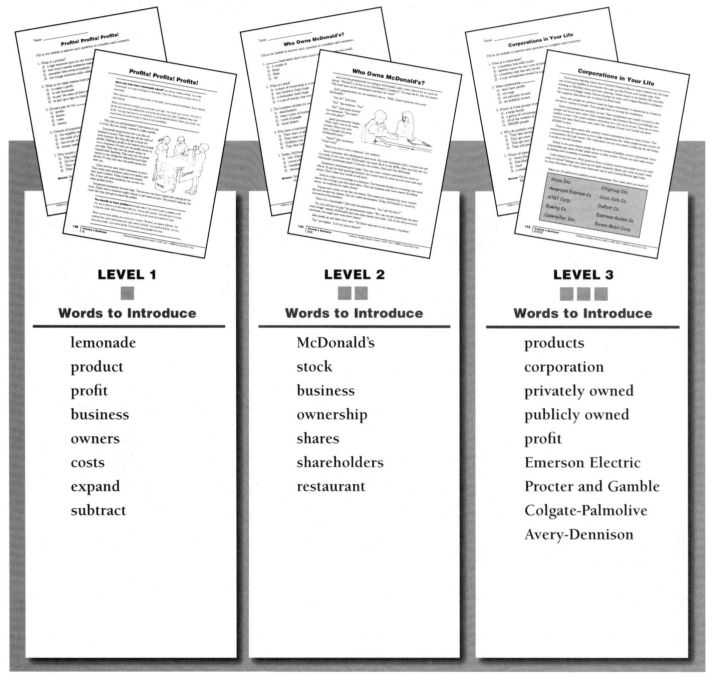

LEVEL 1
Words to Introduce

lemonade

product

profit

business

owners

costs

expand

subtract

LEVEL 2
Words to Introduce

McDonald's

stock

business

ownership

shares

shareholders

restaurant

LEVEL 3
Words to Introduce

products

corporation

privately owned

publicly owned

profit

Emerson Electric

Procter and Gamble

Colgate-Palmolive

Avery-Dennison

Nonfiction Reading Practice, Grade 4 • EMC 3315 • ©2003 by Evan-Moor Corp.

Kinds of Businesses

Grace's Garden Shop

Joe's Gas Station

Rush Hour Convenience Store

Clothing by Design

Which business would you like to own?

Profits! Profits! Profits!

Have you ever had a lemonade stand? You set up a table outside. You write "Lemonade" on a sign and tape it to the table. Then you make your product, which is lemonade.

With cups and a pitcher of lemonade on the table, you're ready for business. Soon, people start buying.

When your pitcher is empty, you pull down your sign. You count your money. You took in $5.00. But you must subtract the cost of the lemonade and cups. Together, they cost $1.00. You pay that back to your parents, so you're left with $4.00. That's your profit. You might save your profit money or use it to buy something.

Why did you sell lemonade? One reason is that it is fun. But you mostly wanted to make a profit.

Lemonade stand owners are a lot like all business owners. They both pay all the costs of their business. But they also get to keep the profits. Making a profit is the reason most people own a business. Owners use the profit money to pay bills. They may use the profit money to expand their business. They may use the profit money to buy things for themselves and their family. Or they may save the profit money for later use.

Some owners want their businesses to grow. They make more products, open new stores, and hire more workers. These things cost money. But, if they sell more products, the owners can make greater profits.

Sometimes businesses become huge. The owners can have a hard time paying all the costs. That's when a business might choose to get more owners. The owners help pay the costs. But they also get to share the profits.

You decide to have another lemonade stand. You want to earn a greater profit. You ask a friend to run the stand with you. You're both owners. You both put in money to pay the costs. With more money, you can buy a lot more lemonade and cups.

When you're done selling, you count your money. This time, you take in $20.00. You subtract the cost of the lemonade and cups, which is $4.00. Your profit is $16.00. You two share the profits. Your half is $8.00. Your profits were greater this time.

Name _____

Profits! Profits! Profits!

Fill in the bubble to answer each question or complete each sentence.

1. What is a *product*?
   - Ⓐ a sign someone puts on her business
   - Ⓑ how much money someone makes
   - Ⓒ someone who owns a business
   - Ⓓ the things someone sells—like lemonade

2. What is the main reason most people own a business?
   - Ⓐ to make a profit
   - Ⓑ to sell lemonade
   - Ⓒ to pay the costs of their business
   - Ⓓ to put up a sign on their business

3. Owners pay all the _____ of a business.
   - Ⓐ profits
   - Ⓑ shares
   - Ⓒ costs
   - Ⓓ money

4. Owners of businesses can make a profit. What is a *profit*?
   - Ⓐ the supplies needed for a business
   - Ⓑ the costs of a business
   - Ⓒ the owner of a business
   - Ⓓ money made from a business

5. Why would a lemonade stand have two or more owners?
   - Ⓐ They can help drink the lemonade.
   - Ⓑ All the owners can chip in money to pay the costs.
   - Ⓒ They will have more fun.
   - Ⓓ They are all friends.

Bonus: Imagine that you have a lemonade stand. On the back of this page, list two things you might do with the profit money you make.

Who Owns McDonald's?

Jack and his grandmother are eating at McDonald's. Jack twirls a french fry in a pool of catsup. "Wouldn't it be fun to own McDonald's, Grandma?" He pops the fry into his mouth. "We could have all the hamburgers and fries we want!"

Jack's grandmother sets her sandwich down. "Well, I know someone who owns McDonald's."

"You do?" Jack asks.

"Yes!" She exclaims. "You!"

"Me?" Jack looks around the restaurant. "You mean I own this place?"

Jack's grandmother laughs. "Well, you're one of the many owners. When you were born, I bought you some McDonald's stock."

"Stock?" Jack questions. "What's that?"

"Stock is a way to own a business," she explains.

Some businesses, like McDonald's, have stock. But most businesses don't, because they are too small. At one time, even McDonald's was small. Back in the 1950s, there was only one tiny McDonald's hamburger stand. It had just two owners, Dick and Mac McDonald.

Sometimes, businesses grow larger. They hire more workers and build new stores or offices. To pay for their growing business, the owners have to come up with more and more money. That's when they decide to sell stock.

Stock is a share of ownership in a business. The business divides its ownership into equal shares, like cutting a pie into equal slices. Then the business sells these shares. By selling shares, the business can make money.

Anyone who wishes to can buy the shares. This means the business has many owners. Because owners buy shares, they are called shareholders. Today, McDonald's is owned by thousands of shareholders.

"Since I'm a shareholder," Jack asks his grandmother, "can I get free food?"

"No, you still have to pay," his grandmother replies. "But you can get something that lasts much longer: money. McDonald's pays you some money each year. And, if you sell your stock sometime, you might earn even more money."

Jack stands up and takes their trays. "We better take care of my business, Grandma."

"Yes," she replies. "Let's buy some dessert!"

Nonfiction Reading Practice, Grade 4 • EMC 3315 • ©2003 by Evan-Moor Corp.

Name _____

Who Owns McDonald's?

Fill in the bubble to answer each question or complete each sentence.

1. _____ businesses don't have stock because they are too small.
   Ⓐ A couple of
   Ⓑ Some
   Ⓒ Most
   Ⓓ All

2. What is a *stock*?
   Ⓐ a share of ownership in a business
   Ⓑ any business that's huge
   Ⓒ a restaurant that's huge
   Ⓓ a type of money that owners have

3. The business divides its ownership into _____.
   Ⓐ shareholders
   Ⓑ many types of businesses
   Ⓒ types of people
   Ⓓ equal shares

4. Why does a business sell shares?
   Ⓐ They want to give away the business to other people.
   Ⓑ They want to make lots of money.
   Ⓒ Children can own stock.
   Ⓓ They like having stock.

5. Today, McDonald's has _____ shareholders.
   Ⓐ two (Dick and Mac)
   Ⓑ twenty-five
   Ⓒ hundreds of
   Ⓓ thousands of

Bonus: On the back of this page, explain why someone would want be a shareholder in a business like McDonald's.

Corporations in Your Life

Each school morning, music from Cherise's Emerson Electric radio awakens her. She hops out of bed and shuffles to the shower. She suds up with Procter and Gamble soap. After dressing in Wal-Mart shoes and Sears clothing, Cherise heads to the kitchen. She munches on a bowl of Kellogg's cereal. Cherise brushes her teeth with Colgate-Palmolive toothpaste. Her neighbor then drives her to school in a Ford truck.

Every day, people use products made by huge corporations. A corporation is a business owned by a group of people. These people share in owning the corporation.

Most corporations are privately owned. These corporations are usually owned by a few people who know each other. Other corporations, like Emerson Electric and Kellogg's, are publicly owned. That means anyone—including you—can be an owner. There are so many owners that most don't know each other. For example, Procter and Gamble has about 200,000 owners.

There is one main reason why publicly owned corporations have so many owners. That reason is money. It's expensive to run a huge corporation. But, when people become owners of a corporation, they pay money. The corporation can use this money to help pay for the things it needs to run the business.

Money is the same reason people like to be owners of publicly owned corporations. Some corporations pay some of their profit money to their owners. Owners can also make money by selling their ownership to someone else.

Look around you now. What products from a publicly owned corporation have you used today at school? Perhaps you typed on an Apple computer. Maybe you wrote on paper made by Avery-Dennison. Or maybe your classroom was lit with General Electric light bulbs.

Alcoa Inc.	Citigroup Inc.
American Express Co.	Coca-Cola Co.
AT&T Corp.	DuPont Co.
Boeing Co.	Eastman Kodak Co.
Caterpillar Inc.	Exxon Mobil Corp.

Here are 10 well-known publicly owned corporations. How many have you heard of?

Nonfiction Reading Practice, Grade 4 • EMC 3315 • ©2003 by Evan-Moor Corp.

Name _____

Corporations in Your Life

Fill in the bubble to answer each question or complete each sentence.

1. What is a *corporation*?
   - Ⓐ a business that sells trucks
   - Ⓑ another name for any type of business
   - Ⓒ a business that has one owner
   - Ⓓ a type of business owned by a group of people

2. Most corporations _____.
   - Ⓐ don't have profits
   - Ⓑ are huge
   - Ⓒ are privately owned
   - Ⓓ are publicly owned

3. Which of these groups of people probably own a private corporation?
   - Ⓐ a large family
   - Ⓑ a group of school-age children
   - Ⓒ all of the workers at Coca-Cola Company
   - Ⓓ 200,000 people

4. Why do publicly owned corporations have so many owners?
   - Ⓐ They like having many people run them.
   - Ⓑ They get more money to use.
   - Ⓒ They get new business ideas from all the owners.
   - Ⓓ They sell products to other people.

5. Which of these businesses is not publicly owned?
   - Ⓐ Avery-Dennison
   - Ⓑ Wal-Mart
   - Ⓒ Ford
   - Ⓓ a small donut shop in your town

Bonus: On the back of this page, explain why corporations like Emerson Electric and Kellogg's are publicly owned.

Ludwig van Beethoven

Introducing the Topic

1. Reproduce page 135 for individual students, or make a transparency to use with a group or the whole class.

2. Read and discuss with students the time line of Ludwig van Beethoven's life. Point out that even though he became deaf, Beethoven composed some of the greatest musical works in history.

Reading the Selections

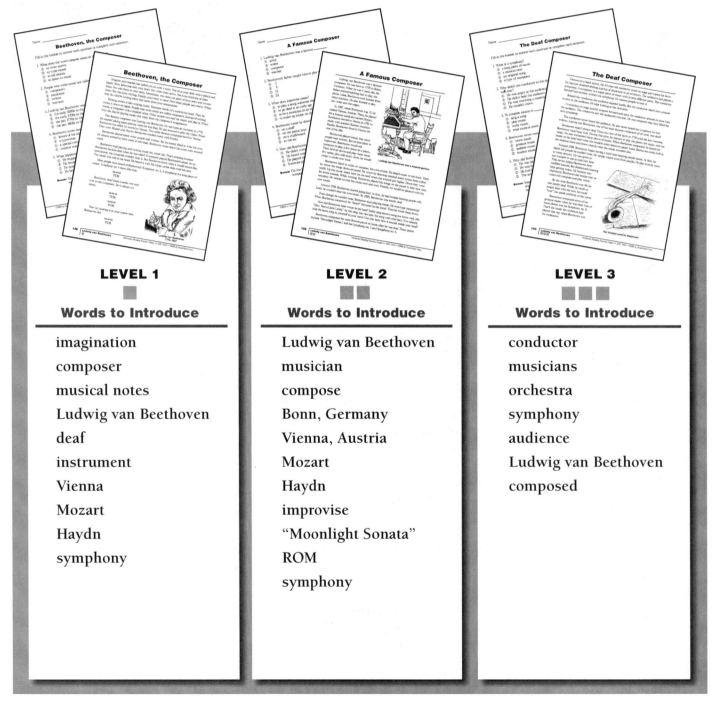

LEVEL 1
⬛
Words to Introduce

imagination

composer

musical notes

Ludwig van Beethoven

deaf

instrument

Vienna

Mozart

Haydn

symphony

LEVEL 2
⬛ ⬛
Words to Introduce

Ludwig van Beethoven

musician

compose

Bonn, Germany

Vienna, Austria

Mozart

Haydn

improvise

"Moonlight Sonata"

ROM

symphony

LEVEL 3
⬛ ⬛ ⬛
Words to Introduce

conductor

musicians

orchestra

symphony

audience

Ludwig van Beethoven

composed

Nonfiction Reading Practice, Grade 4 • EMC 3315 • ©2003 by Evan-Moor Corp.

Time Line of Ludwig van Beethoven

1770 — Born in Bonn, Germany.

1774 — Started to learn to play piano and violin from his father.

1782 — By age 12, had written and published piano sonatas.

1787 — Played for Mozart, who said Beethoven would "soon astonish the world."

1792 — Moved to Vienna to study with Joseph Haydn.

1795 — Gave first public concert; considered gifted concert pianist.

1800 — Composed the first of nine symphonies; was losing his hearing.

1808 — Wrote Symphony no. 5, one of his most famous works.

1815 — Wrote six symphonies, fourteen piano sonatas, one opera, and many chamber music works by this time.

1820 — Became totally deaf; continued to write and perform.

1824 — Completed Symphony no. 9.

1827 — Died in Vienna; an estimated 10,000 people watched the funeral procession.

Beethoven, the Composer

Imagine your teacher has asked you to write a story. You sit at your desk with a pencil and paper. Story ideas pop into your head. You write them down. You keep thinking of more ideas. You add them to your story. Sometimes, you cross out parts of your story and rewrite them. But you keep writing. Finally, your story is done. Now other people can read it. When they do, they're reading ideas that came from your imagination.

Writing stories is like writing music. Someone thinks of a tune in his head. Then he writes it down on paper. People who write music are called composers. Instead of writing words, a composer writes musical notes. Other people can read the music and play it. When they do, they're playing music that came from the composer's imagination.

One famous composer was Ludwig van Beethoven. He was born in Germany in 1770. He started taking piano lessons when he was four. He also learned to play the violin. When Beethoven was older, he moved to Vienna. Two other famous composers lived in Vienna. They were Mozart and Haydn. Beethoven studied music with Haydn.

Beethoven played music other people had written. But he mostly liked to write his own. He always seemed to have tunes in his head. Beethoven wrote down his tunes with musical notes.

Beethoven kept playing and writing music his whole life. That's amazing because Beethoven became deaf when he was older! If someone played Beethoven's music on an instrument, the composer couldn't hear it. But Beethoven knew what it would sound like. The music was still in his head. He heard it with his mind, rather than with his ears.

Most people have heard of Beethoven's Symphony no. 5. A symphony is a long piece of music. Symphony no. 5 starts like this:

>**ta-ta-ta**
>
>TUM

Beethoven used these sounds over and over in his symphony. Say it aloud two times.

>**ta-ta-ta**
>
>TUM

>**ta-ta-ta**
>
>TUM

Now try hearing it in your mind—like Beethoven did.

>**ta-ta-ta**
>
>TUM

**Ludwig van Beethoven
1770–1827**

Nonfiction Reading Practice, Grade 4 • EMC 3315 • ©2003 by Evan-Moor Corp.

Beethoven, the Composer

Fill in the bubble to answer each question or complete each sentence.

1. What does the word *compose* mean in this article?
   - Ⓐ to write poetry
   - Ⓑ to write music
   - Ⓒ to tell stories
   - Ⓓ to listen to music

2. People who write music are called _____.
   - Ⓐ composers
   - Ⓑ musicians
   - Ⓒ writers
   - Ⓓ teachers

3. Ludwig van Beethoven was a famous composer from _____.
   - Ⓐ the early 1600s to the late 1700s
   - Ⓑ the early 1700s to the late 1800s
   - Ⓒ the late 1770s to the early 1800s
   - Ⓓ the late 1800s to the early 1900s

4. Beethoven wrote down his songs with _____.
   - Ⓐ letters of the alphabet
   - Ⓑ a typewriter
   - Ⓒ a special computer
   - Ⓓ musical notes

5. What happened to Beethoven when he was older?
   - Ⓐ He stopped playing music.
   - Ⓑ He became deaf.
   - Ⓒ He quit writing music.
   - Ⓓ He became blind.

Bonus: On the back of this page, explain how Beethoven was able to compose music even when he couldn't hear it.

A Famous Composer

Ludwig van Beethoven was a famous composer. He was born in 1770 in Bonn, Germany. When he was 4 years old, his father started teaching him to play the piano. Later, Beethoven took lessons from other teachers. He also learned to play the violin and the organ.

In 1787, when Beethoven was 17, he visited Vienna, Austria. There, he played for a famous musician named Mozart. Beethoven moved to Vienna in 1792 to study with another famous musician, Haydn. Beethoven lived in Vienna the rest of his life.

Beethoven played music that other people had written. But he also liked to improvise. Beethoven would ask someone to play a few notes on a piano. Then he'd sit down and play those same few notes, plus add more. Soon, he would create a whole new tune.

Ludwig van Beethoven was a musical genius.

Beethoven liked to write, or compose, his own music. He heard music in his head. Then he wrote the songs down on paper. He wrote by drawing musical notes across lines called staffs. Up the music notes went on the staff when the sounds got higher. Down they went for lower sounds. While writing, Beethoven played his songs on the piano to hear how they sounded. He would rewrite his music over and over. Finally, he would be pleased with his new music.

Around 1798, Beethoven started going deaf. At first, he had trouble hearing people talk. Later, he couldn't hear his own music. By 1820, Beethoven was totally deaf.

Even though he couldn't hear, Beethoven kept playing music. He even kept composing! When Beethoven composed, he "heard" the tunes in his mind. Then he wrote them down.

How did Beethoven hear music in his head? Softly sing aloud a song you know well, like "Mary Had a Little Lamb." As you sing, you can hear the song with your ears. Now silently sing the same song to yourself in your mind. Can you hear how it sounds inside your head?

Beethoven composed his most famous pieces of music after he was deaf. These pieces include "Moonlight Sonata" and his Symphony no. 5 and Symphony no. 9.

Nonfiction Reading Practice, Grade 4 • EMC 3315 • ©2003 by Evan-Moor Corp.

A Famous Composer

1. Ludwig van Beethoven was a famous _____.
   - Ⓐ artist
   - Ⓑ writer
   - Ⓒ composer
   - Ⓓ teacher

2. Beethoven's father taught him to play the piano when he was _____ years old.
   - Ⓐ 2
   - Ⓑ 4
   - Ⓒ 12
   - Ⓓ 22

3. What does *improvise* mean?
   - Ⓐ to play a song someone else wrote
   - Ⓑ to go deaf at an early age
   - Ⓒ to be a musician in an orchestra
   - Ⓓ to make up music on the spur of the moment

4. Beethoven wrote by drawing musical notes _____.
   - Ⓐ on a staff
   - Ⓑ on the piano keys
   - Ⓒ on a chalkboard
   - Ⓓ in the air

5. How did Beethoven compose after he was deaf?
   - Ⓐ He didn't compose when he was deaf.
   - Ⓑ He heard tunes in his head and wrote them down.
   - Ⓒ He played the piano, and someone else wrote the notes.
   - Ⓓ Someone played the piano, and he wrote the notes.

Bonus: On the back of this page, explain why you think Beethoven kept composing even after he couldn't hear anymore.

The Deaf Composer

Dressed in a black jacket, the 54-year-old conductor stood on stage and wiped his brow. He had just finished leading a group of musicians in an orchestra. The orchestra had played a symphony. A symphony is a major piece of music with several different parts. The conductor himself had recently written the symphony. He wanted people to hear it.

Behind the conductor, the audience clapped loudly. But the conductor didn't turn around to bow to the audience. He kept looking at the orchestra.

A musician on stage quickly stepped forward and spun the conductor around to show him the audience. The conductor saw the audience's reaction. He was overjoyed that they liked his new symphony.

The conductor never heard the audience. He also never heard the symphony he had written. Ludwig van Beethoven, one of the most famous composers of all time, was deaf!

Beethoven wasn't always deaf. From the time of his birth in 1770 until his late twenties, Beethoven could hear well. During this time, he learned to play the piano, the organ, and the violin. He also composed many pieces of music. When Beethoven composed, he heard the music in his head and wrote the musical notes down on paper. Later, Beethoven could look at the musical notes and know exactly what the music sounded like.

Around 1798, Beethoven began having a hard time hearing people speak. At first, he didn't tell people he couldn't hear. He simply stayed away from people. He also secretly went to many doctors. He was given an ear trumpet to use to help him hear. This device helped Beethoven hear muffled sounds. But Beethoven's hearing kept getting worse. He became very depressed. Beethoven did realize that he could still compose and play music.

By the time Beethoven was 50, he was totally deaf. While he could no longer hear with his ears, he could "hear" the music perfectly in his mind.

Beethoven composed some of his greatest music when he was deaf. One of these pieces was his Symphony no. 9. That's the music the orchestra had played that day when Beethoven was the conductor.

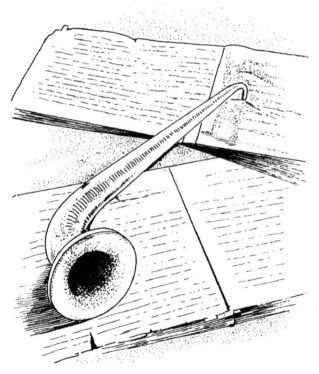

Ear trumpet used by Beethoven

Nonfiction Reading Practice, Grade 4 • EMC 3315 • ©2003 by Evan-Moor Corp.

The Deaf Composer

Fill in the bubble to answer each question or complete each sentence.

1. What is a *symphony*?
   - Ⓐ a long piece of music
   - Ⓑ a musical note
   - Ⓒ an original song
   - Ⓓ a type of composer

2. Why didn't the conductor in the story turn around when the symphony was over?
   - Ⓐ He was angry at the audience.
   - Ⓑ He didn't hear the audience clapping.
   - Ⓒ He was watching a musician playing a solo.
   - Ⓓ He couldn't move.

3. To *compose* means to _____.
   - Ⓐ sing a song
   - Ⓑ play music
   - Ⓒ write music
   - Ⓓ read musical notes

4. Beethoven wrote some of his _____ when he was deaf.
   - Ⓐ worst music
   - Ⓑ greatest music
   - Ⓒ saddest music
   - Ⓓ loudest music

5. Why did Beethoven become deaf?
   - Ⓐ He was hit in the head.
   - Ⓑ He was born that way.
   - Ⓒ He had listened to loud music too long.
   - Ⓓ The article didn't say.

Bonus: Imagine you were Beethoven and that you loved music. On the back of this page, explain how you would feel if you became deaf and couldn't hear music anymore.

Drawing

Introducing the Topic

1. Reproduce page 143 for individual students.

2. Provide each student or small group of students with a real object or collection of real objects (such as a vase of flowers, a bowl of fruit, or items on a desk) to use as a model for drawing a picture on the top half of the paper. Do not give them any instructions as to how to draw the objects. Afterward, have students share their drawings. Ask them how they approached the task and what was difficult about the process.

Tell them they will find out about a way that artists draw that helps them create realistic pictures. After students have finished the unit about drawing, have them draw the same objects on the bottom of the page. Discuss how their approach to the task of drawing changed or improved.

Reading the Selections

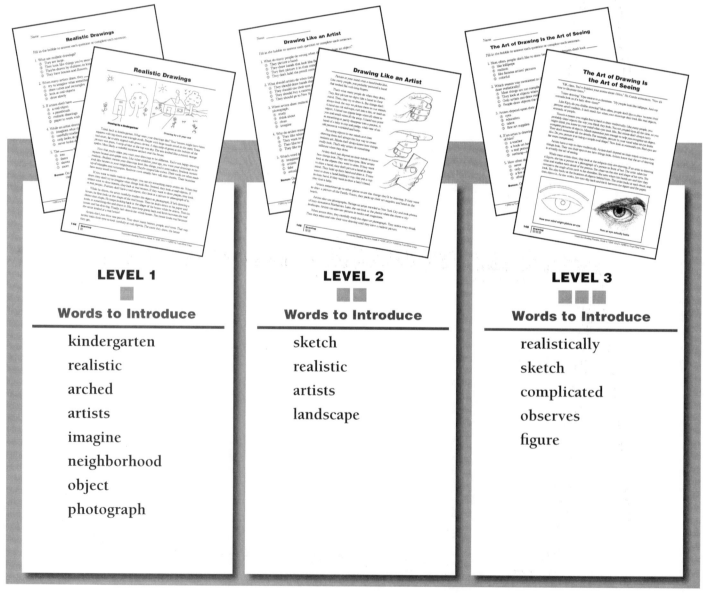

LEVEL 1
◼

Words to Introduce

kindergarten

realistic

arched

artists

imagine

neighborhood

object

photograph

LEVEL 2
◼ ◼

Words to Introduce

sketch

realistic

artists

landscape

LEVEL 3
◼ ◼ ◼

Words to Introduce

realistically

sketch

complicated

observes

figure

Nonfiction Reading Practice, Grade 4 • EMC 3315 • ©2003 by Evan-Moor Corp.

Drawing Before Reading the Unit

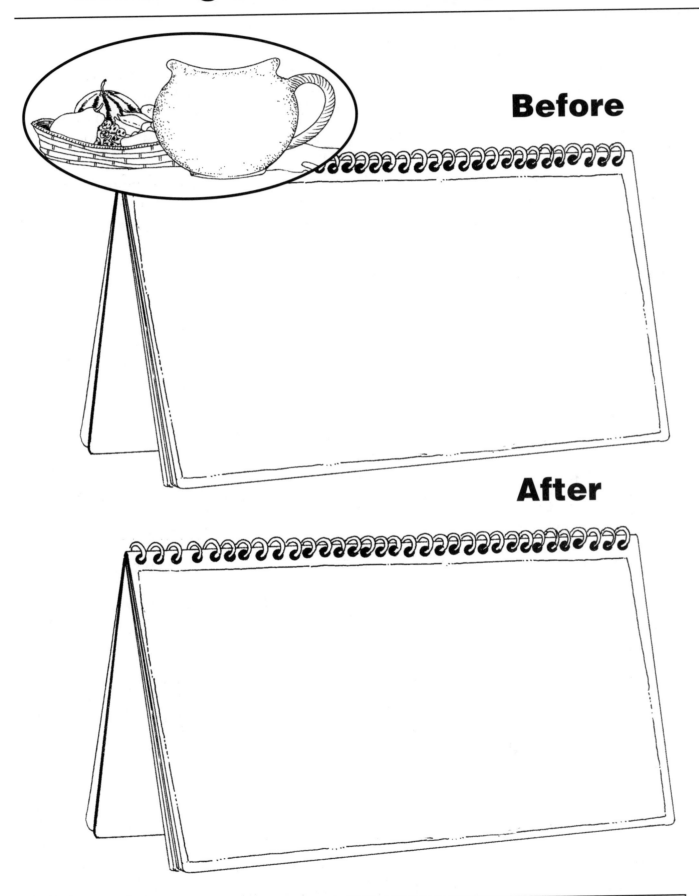

Before

After

Realistic Drawings

Drawing by a kindergartner   Drawing by a 9-year-old

Think back to kindergarten. What were your drawings like? Your houses might have been squares with big doors and triangle roofs. People with large heads stood in the yard. Trees had short, fat trunks topped with green circles. A thin strip of green at the bottom of the picture was grass. A strip of blue at the top was sky. The sun looked like a round, orange spider. Most likely, a colorful rainbow arched over the house.

Now that you're older, you want your drawings to be different. You're not happy drawing square houses and spider suns. Like other children your age, you want your drawings to be realistic. *Realistic* means your drawings look like things you've seen before. Realistic houses look like houses in your neighborhood. They're shaped like cubes. Their roofs are often made up of triangles and rectangles. Realistic trees usually have tall, thin trunks. Their branches have many small leaves.

If you want to make realistic drawings, you can try something many artists do. When they draw, they don't try to imagine what things look like. Instead, they look at real objects. If artists want to draw houses, they look at real houses. If they want to draw people, they look at real people. If artists don't have a real object, they look at a picture or photograph of it.

While he draws, the artist carefully studies the object or photograph. If he's drawing a house, he first looks at the shape of the real house. Then he looks down at his paper and draws that shape. He keeps looking back at the shape of the house while he draws. Then he looks at something else and draws it. His eyes keep going back and forth between the real house and his drawing. Finally, he's drawn the whole house. The house looks real because the artist looked at a real house!

Artists don't just draw one picture. They draw many houses, people, and trees. That way, artists train their eyes to look carefully at real objects. The more they draw, the better they get.

Name _____

Realistic Drawings

Fill in the bubble to answer each question or complete each sentence.

1. What are *realistic drawings*?
   - Ⓐ They are large.
   - Ⓑ They look like things you've seen before.
   - Ⓒ They're drawn by children in kindergarten.
   - Ⓓ They have houses and flowers.

2. When many artists draw, they _____.
   - Ⓐ try to imagine what something looks like
   - Ⓑ draw cubes and rectangles
   - Ⓒ look at real objects
   - Ⓓ draw slowly

3. If artists don't have _____, they can look at a picture or photo of it.
   - Ⓐ a real object
   - Ⓑ a paintbrush
   - Ⓒ realistic drawings
   - Ⓓ paper to work with

4. While an artist draws a realistic picture, he _____.
   - Ⓐ imagines what things look like
   - Ⓑ carefully studies the object or photo
   - Ⓒ only looks at photos
   - Ⓓ never looks down at the paper

5. The _____ artists draw, the better they get.
   - Ⓐ less
   - Ⓑ faster
   - Ⓒ slower
   - Ⓓ more

Bonus: On the back of this page, explain why artists look at real objects when they draw.

Drawing Like an Artist

Picture in your mind what a hand looks like. Like many people, you probably pictured a hand that looked flat with long fingers.

That's what many people do when they draw. They first picture an object like a hand in their mind. Then, they try to draw it. But things don't always look the way we picture them in our minds. A hand can tilt sideways, curl into a fist, or hold an object. A hand can appear large when it's close to you and small when it's far away. A hand can point at something or partly disappear into a pocket. A hand of a baby is tiny and pudgy, while one of an old person is wrinkled and bony.

Picturing objects in our minds and then drawing them isn't always the best way to create realistic art. Minds don't always know how things really look. That's why artists do something different when they draw.

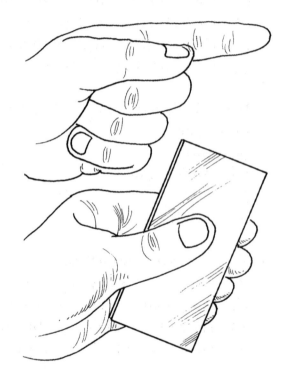

Artists don't just depend on their minds to know how things look. They use their eyes. Most artists look at the objects they want to draw. If they want to draw a hand, they don't picture a hand in their mind. They hold up their hand and draw it. If they want to draw a hand holding a cup, they put a cup in their hand. If they want to draw a baby's hand, they find a baby.

Artists sometimes go to other places to see the things they'll be drawing. If they want to draw a picture of the Pacific Ocean, they pack up their art supplies and head to the beach.

Artists also use photographs. Perhaps an artist traveled to New York City and took photos of busy downtown Manhattan. Later, she can look at the photos when she draws a city landscape. Artists can also use pictures in books and magazines.

When artists draw, they carefully study the object or photograph. They notice every detail. Then they relax and take their time drawing until they have a realistic picture.

Name _____

Drawing Like an Artist

Fill in the bubble to answer each question or complete each sentence.

1. What do many people do wrong when they try to draw an object?
   - Ⓐ They picture a hand.
   - Ⓑ They draw hands that look like fists.
   - Ⓒ They first picture it in their minds, and then they draw it.
   - Ⓓ They don't hold the pencil correctly.

2. What should artists do when they draw realistic pictures?
   - Ⓐ They should draw hands that look flat.
   - Ⓑ They should use their eyes and look at objects carefully.
   - Ⓒ They should buy a camera to take pictures.
   - Ⓓ They should go to New York City to study.

3. When artists draw realistic pictures, they carefully _____ the object or photograph.
   - Ⓐ study
   - Ⓑ think about
   - Ⓒ clean
   - Ⓓ imagine

4. Why do artists sometimes use photographs?
   - Ⓐ They like taking pictures.
   - Ⓑ They want to see how something looks.
   - Ⓒ They like to make a collection of pictures.
   - Ⓓ They like to look at Manhattan.

5. Which word is a synonym for *realistic*?
   - Ⓐ imaginary
   - Ⓑ artistic
   - Ⓒ fake
   - Ⓓ actual

Bonus: On the back of this page, explain how artists use their eyes when they draw.

The Art of Drawing Is the Art of Seeing

"OK, class. You've finished your stories about Africa," Mr. Combs announces. "Now it's time to illustrate them."

"I hate drawing," Kiyo moans to a classmate. "My people look like lollipops. And my animals look as if a baby drew them!"

Like Kiyo, do you dislike drawing? Most often, people don't like to draw because their pictures aren't realistic. It isn't much fun when your drawings don't look like real objects, animals, or people.

There's a reason you might find it hard to draw realistically. Like many people, you probably draw objects the way you think they look. You see people's eyes all the time, so you might think you know in your mind what eyes look like. But minds don't always carry complete pictures of objects. Minds remember just enough to help you recognize an object. They don't remember all the details. For example, picture in your mind what an eye looks like. Do you picture it as being a simple oval shape? Now look at someone's eye. Real eyes are far more complicated.

Artists have a way to draw realistically. Artists don't depend on their minds to know how things look. They use their eyes to see how things look. Artists know that the art of drawing is actually the art of seeing.

While most artists draw, they look at the subjects they are drawing. If an artist is drawing a figure, she has a person or a photograph of a person in front of her. The artist takes her time and studies each detail of the person. She observes the size and shape of his eyes. She compares the angle of his neck to his shoulder. She sees where his hands are and how they look. She also looks at the locations of objects behind him. The artist looks at each detail, and then draws it. As she works, her eyes slip back and forth between the figure and the paper.

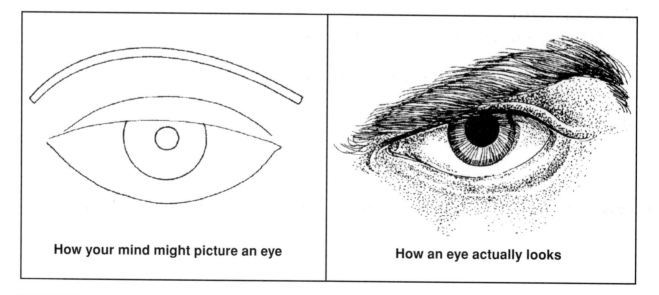

How your mind might picture an eye   How an eye actually looks

Nonfiction Reading Practice, Grade 4 • EMC 3315 • ©2003 by Evan-Moor Corp.

Name _____

The Art of Drawing Is the Art of Seeing

Fill in the bubble to answer each question or complete each sentence.

1. Most often, people don't like to draw because their pictures don't look _____.
   - Ⓐ like lollipops
   - Ⓑ realistic
   - Ⓒ like famous artists' pictures
   - Ⓓ colorful

2. Which reason was mentioned in the article for why people find it hard to draw realistically?
   - Ⓐ Most things are too complicated to draw.
   - Ⓑ They look at objects when they draw.
   - Ⓒ Only artists can draw realistically.
   - Ⓓ People draw objects the way they think they should look.

3. Artists depend upon their _____, not their minds, when they draw.
   - Ⓐ eyes
   - Ⓑ education
   - Ⓒ talent
   - Ⓓ fine art supplies

4. If an artist is drawing a person, what does the artist usually have in front of him?
   - Ⓐ a teacher
   - Ⓑ a book on how to draw
   - Ⓒ a real person or photo of a person
   - Ⓓ nothing—he just uses his imagination to draw

5. How often does an artist look at the object she is drawing?
   - Ⓐ never
   - Ⓑ only once
   - Ⓒ a few times
   - Ⓓ often

Bonus: On the back of this page, explain what this means: "The art of drawing is the art of seeing."

Acting

Introducing the Topic

1. Reproduce page 151 for individual students, or make a transparency to use with a group or the whole class.

2. Show students the picture. Read and talk about what is happening in the play. Discuss with students any experiences they've had being in a play, or any plays they've seen. What was the play about? What did they enjoy about the play?

Reading the Selections

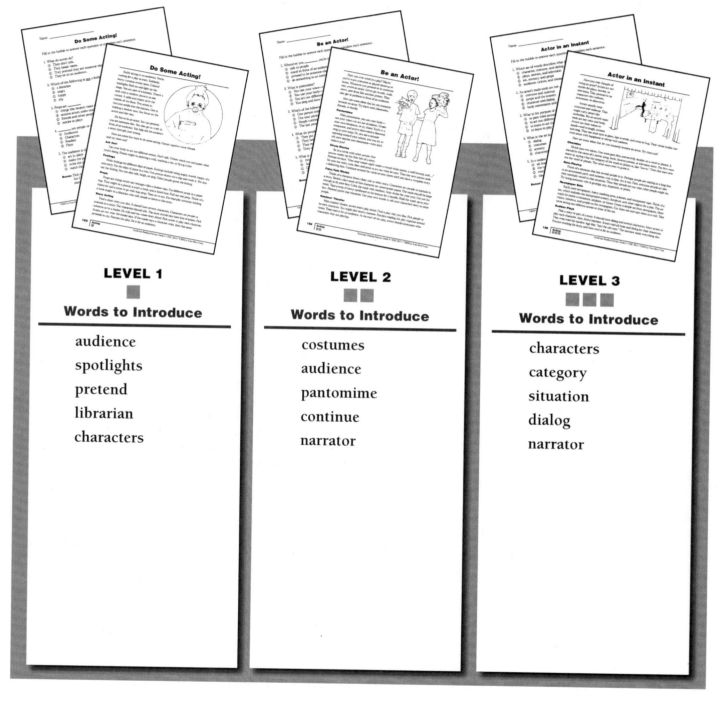

LEVEL 1	LEVEL 2	LEVEL 3
Words to Introduce	**Words to Introduce**	**Words to Introduce**
audience	costumes	characters
spotlights	audience	category
pretend	pantomime	situation
librarian	continue	dialog
characters	narrator	narrator

Nonfiction Reading Practice, Grade 4 • EMC 3315 • ©2003 by Evan-Moor Corp.

Acting in a Play

The children built the set to look like a house. The set includes the scenery, furniture, and other objects on the stage for the play.

The children painted the *scenery* on the backdrop. They painted curtains and a fireplace.

Three *actors* are onstage right now. They are pretending to be the *characters* of an old woman, a young man, and a cat. The actors are wearing *costumes*.

The *audience* is enjoying the play.

Do Some Acting!

You're sitting in an audience. You're waiting for a play to start. Suddenly, heavy curtains sweep open. Colored spotlights flick on and light up the stage. You see part of a kitchen. There's a sink with a window above it in one corner. A table and chairs sit in the middle of the floor. Two actors in costume stride into the kitchen. One is holding a broken vase. You focus on the actors and the vase.

It's fun to be an actor. You can pretend you are someone else. You also get to work in front of an audience. You help tell the audience a story through your acting.

Here are some fun ways to do some acting. Gather together some friends and try them out!

Act Out!

Use your body to act out different events. Don't talk. Others watch you and guess what you're doing. Events might be painting a wall, washing a car, or flying a kite.

Feelings

Write feelings on different slips of paper. Feelings include being angry, scared, happy, shy, and sorry. Put the slips of paper in a box. One person draws out a slip and reads it. She acts out the feeling. She can also talk, laugh, or sing. Other people guess the feeling.

Props

Props are things actors use onstage—like a broken vase. Put different props in a paper bag. They might be a pencil, a scarf, a book, and a lunch box. Pull out one prop. Think of a character and a scene to go with that prop. Then act it out. For example, someone holding a book might be a librarian who tells people to listen to the story.

Story Acting

Find a short story you like. It should have several characters. Characters are people or animals in a story. The characters should talk. The story should also have lots of action. Pick someone to be a reader. He will read the whole story aloud. Pick actors to play each character. Actors act out what the reader says. If the reader says a character cries, then that actor pretends to cry. Practice the play. Do it for an audience.

Name _____

Do Some Acting!

Fill in the bubble to answer each question or complete each sentence.

1. What do actors do?
   - Ⓐ They don't talk.
   - Ⓑ They break vases.
   - Ⓒ They pretend they are someone else.
   - Ⓓ They sit in an audience.

2. Which of the following is not a feeling?
   - Ⓐ a librarian
   - Ⓑ angry
   - Ⓒ happy
   - Ⓓ shy

3. *Props* are _____.
   - Ⓐ things like broken vases that actors use onstage
   - Ⓑ actions actors make onstage
   - Ⓒ friends and other people who come to see the play
   - Ⓓ stories in plays

4. _____ are people or animals in a story.
   - Ⓐ Audiences
   - Ⓑ Characters
   - Ⓒ Readers
   - Ⓓ Plays

5. The audience is the people who _____.
   - Ⓐ act in plays
   - Ⓑ make the props in plays
   - Ⓒ write the plays
   - Ⓓ watch the plays

Bonus: Pick one of the ways to do some acting described in this article: Act Out!, Feelings, Props, or Story Acting. On the back of this page, name the one you would like to try and explain why.

Be an Actor!

Have you ever acted in a play? Maybe you've worn costumes or played dress-up at home. Whenever you pretend to be someone else, you're an actor. Actors get to talk, walk, move, and dress like another person. They also get to perform in front of an audience.

Here are some ideas that let you instantly become an actor. Try them with classmates, friends, or family.

Pantomime

With pantomime, you use your body—not your voice—to act out situations. Create your own situations, or try these: You're at a restaurant, and you've discovered a diamond ring in your soup. Or, you see a tornado spinning toward your school, and you try to tell your teacher and classmates—who don't believe you!

Circle Stories

Sit in a circle with other people. One person makes up the first line of a story. Perhaps he says, "One clear winter night under a round white moon, a wolf howled, and…." He uses his voice, eyes, face, and arms to act out what he says. Then the next person adds a following line. Continue around the circle several times until you have a complete story.

Fairy-Tale Masks

Think of a character from a fairy tale or other story. Characters are people or animals in a story. Sketch a face mask of that character on construction paper. The mask should be large enough to fit your face. Color the mask with markers. Snip circles for your eyes. Cut out the mask. Tape a strip of heavy cardboard to the bottom for a handle. Hold the mask up to your face. Pretend you're that character. Use your own words to tell your character's story to other people.

Readers' Theater

With readers' theater, actors read a play aloud. Find a play that you like. Pick people to be each character. You might also need a narrator. Practice reading the play together several times. Then read it for an audience. At the start of the play, actors should announce what characters they are playing.

Nonfiction Reading Practice, Grade 4 • EMC 3315 • ©2003 by Evan-Moor Corp.

Name _____

Be an Actor!

Fill in the bubble to answer each question or complete each sentence.

1. Whenever you _____, you're an actor.
   Ⓐ talk to people
   Ⓑ stand in front of an audience
   Ⓒ pretend to be someone else
   Ⓓ do something in an instant

2. What is *pantomime*?
   Ⓐ You use your voice—not your body—to act out situations.
   Ⓑ You use your body—not your voice—to act out situations.
   Ⓒ You act out different situations.
   Ⓓ You sing and have people figure out the situation.

3. Which of the following is <u>not</u> part of doing a circle story?
   Ⓐ One person makes up the first line of a story and acts it out.
   Ⓑ The next person adds a following line.
   Ⓒ People continue adding lines.
   Ⓓ The last person stands up and tells the whole story.

4. What do people do with the fairy-tale masks?
   Ⓐ They put them on puppets and do puppet shows.
   Ⓑ They hold them to their faces and pretend to be that character.
   Ⓒ They read stories aloud and the audience holds up the masks.
   Ⓓ They wear them while they do pantomime.

5. What is *readers' theater*?
   Ⓐ Actors read a play aloud.
   Ⓑ Actors perform in a large theater.
   Ⓒ One actor plays all the characters in the play.
   Ⓓ The audience helps read the story.

Bonus: On the back of this page, describe how you would pantomime making a peanut butter and jelly sandwich.

Actor in an Instant

Have you ever thought of being an actor? Actors act out stories for plays, movies, or television. They pretend to be characters like robbers, princesses, or detectives.

Actors usually wear costumes and makeup. They might carry props like umbrellas. But an actor's main tools are her voice and body. Actors use their voices to speak—and to laugh, scream, and sing. They use their eyes to glare, lips to smile, and arms to hug. Their whole bodies can twirl about with happiness or droop with sadness.

Here are some ideas that let you instantly become an actor. Try them out!

Charades

Divide into two teams. One team goes first and secretly decides on a word or phrase. It should be the name of a movie, song, book, famous person, or television show. The first team starts by saying what the category of the word or phrase is, like "movie." Then that team acts out the word or phrase. The other team tries to guess it.

Role-Playing

Think of a situation that has several people in it. Perhaps people are waiting in a long line at an amusement park, and someone cuts in line. Act it out. First, everyone should act like they normally would in that situation. Then they should act out what other people might do. Try being someone who is grumpy, shy, impatient, or polite.

Newspaper Sets

You'll need newspapers, heavy marking pens, scissors, and transparent tape. Think of a set, which includes the background scenery, furniture, and other objects for a play. The set might be inside a restaurant, airplane, or house. Create a simple set from newspapers. Draw chairs, windows, and people on the newspapers. Cut them out and tape them to a wall. Take turns acting out different scenes in front of the set.

Sudden Plays

Pick a story or part of a story. It should have dialog and several characters. Select actors to play each character. Also, find a narrator. Actors read all lines and dialog for their characters. They even read the speaker tags like, "said the old man." The narrator reads everything else. Practice reading the story, and then read it for an audience.

Nonfiction Reading Practice, Grade 4 • EMC 3315 • ©2003 by Evan-Moor Corp.

Name _____

Actor in an Instant

Fill in the bubble to answer each question or complete each sentence.

1. Which set of words describes what it's like to be an actor?
   - Ⓐ character, costume, and dialog
   - Ⓑ plays, movies, and television
   - Ⓒ set, scenery, and props
   - Ⓓ audience, tickets, and theater

2. An actor's main tools are her _____.
   - Ⓐ costume and makeup
   - Ⓑ props and the scenery
   - Ⓒ character and dialog
   - Ⓓ body movements and vocal qualities

3. What is the purpose of role-playing?
   - Ⓐ to pass roles around between actors so they get to know each other
   - Ⓑ to act out different types of situations
   - Ⓒ to learn to act things out without saying anything
   - Ⓓ to learn to play like a child

4. What is the *set* in a play?
   - Ⓐ dialog
   - Ⓑ costumes
   - Ⓒ scenery
   - Ⓓ characters

5. In a *sudden play,* the actors read _____.
   - Ⓐ all lines and dialog for their characters, as well as speaker tags
   - Ⓑ the cards that the narrator holds up
   - Ⓒ everything the narrator reads
   - Ⓓ the play suddenly

Bonus: On the back of this page, describe how you would act out this situation: You're a shy person standing onstage in front of a large audience. You tell the audience something about yourself. Describe the same situation as if you were a grumpy person.

Julia Morgan

Introducing the Topic

1. Reproduce page 159 for individual students, or make a transparency to use with a group or the whole class.

2. Read and discuss the time line of Julia Morgan's life, emphasizing the fact that few women in her lifetime achieved so much in the field of architecture. Invite students to pretend they are architects, and have them design the exterior of their dream home on a piece of drawing paper. Then have students share their drawings with the class.

Reading the Selections

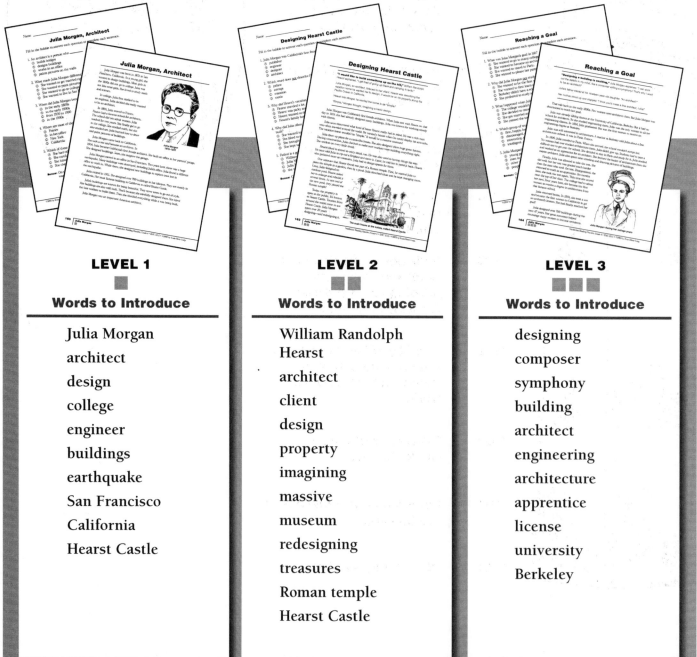

LEVEL 1
■

Words to Introduce

Julia Morgan

architect

design

college

engineer

buildings

earthquake

San Francisco

California

Hearst Castle

LEVEL 2
■ ■

Words to Introduce

William Randolph Hearst

architect

client

design

property

imagining

massive

museum

redesigning

treasures

Roman temple

Hearst Castle

LEVEL 3
■ ■ ■

Words to Introduce

designing

composer

symphony

building

architect

engineering

architecture

apprentice

license

university

Berkeley

Time Line of Julia Morgan's Life

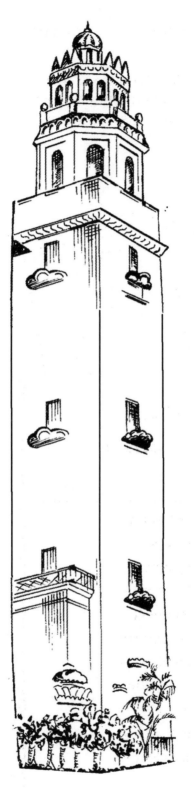

1872 — Born in San Francisco, California.

1890 — Graduated from high school.

1894 — First woman to graduate from the University of California with a degree in civil engineering.

1896 — Traveled to Paris, France, to work and study architecture.

1902 — First woman to graduate from a Paris school with a degree in architecture.

1904 — First woman in California to receive an architect's license.

1906 — Redesigned the Fairmont Hotel and many other buildings after the San Francisco earthquake.

1919 — Hired by William Randolph Hearst to build Hearst Castle, her most famous work.

1939 — Finished working on Hearst Castle.

1951 — Retired after designing over 700 buildings.

1957 — Died at the age of 85.

Julia Morgan, Architect

Julia Morgan was born in 1872 in San Francisco, California. As a young girl, she wanted to design buildings. Most girls in the 1800s did not go to college. Julia was not like most girls. She loved to study math and science.

In college, Julia first studied to be an engineer. Julia decided she really wanted to be an architect.

In 1896, Julia moved to France. France had a famous school for architects. The school did not admit women. Julia worked for two years. She finally got to go to the college. She studied math, but she also studied art. Julia learned how to draw and paint pictures of buildings.

Julia Morgan
1872–1957

Julia Morgan came back to California. She took a test and became an architect. In 1904, Julia became California's first female architect. She built an office in her parents' garage. She designed buildings. Soon, she outgrew the garage.

Julia Morgan moved to an office in San Francisco. Two years later, there was a huge earthquake. Many buildings were destroyed, including Julia's office. Julia found a different office to work in. While there, she designed new buildings to replace ones lost in the earthquake.

Julia retired in 1951. She designed over 700 buildings in her lifetime. They are mostly in California. Her most famous building in California is called Hearst Castle.

Julia's buildings are known for being beautiful. They never seem to go out of style. Her buildings are also well built. That's because she carefully designed them. She hired the best workers to build them. Then she checked everything while it was being built.

Julia Morgan was an important American architect.

Name _____

Julia Morgan, Architect

Fill in the bubble to answer each question or complete each sentence.

1. An *architect* is a person who _____.
   - Ⓐ builds bridges
   - Ⓑ designs buildings
   - Ⓒ works in an office
   - Ⓓ paints pictures on the walls

2. What made Julia Morgan different from most girls of the late 1800s?
   - Ⓐ She wanted to get married right after high school.
   - Ⓑ She wanted to paint pictures of people in France.
   - Ⓒ She wanted to go to college to study architecture.
   - Ⓓ She wanted to live in San Francisco.

3. When did Julia Morgan become an architect?
   - Ⓐ in the early 1800s
   - Ⓑ in the early 1900s
   - Ⓒ from 1950 to 1990
   - Ⓓ in the 1990s

4. Where are most of the buildings that Julia Morgan designed?
   - Ⓐ France
   - Ⓑ in her office
   - Ⓒ New York
   - Ⓓ California

5. Which of these is <u>not</u> a reason why Julia Morgan's buildings are well built?
   - Ⓐ She had other engineers design her buildings.
   - Ⓑ She carefully designed the buildings.
   - Ⓒ She hired the best workers to build the buildings.
   - Ⓓ She checked everything while the buildings were being built.

Bonus: On the back of this page, describe what kind of architect Julia Morgan was.

Designing Hearst Castle

"I would like to build something up on the hill," William Randolph Hearst explained. "I get tired of going up there and camping in tents."

Julia Morgan, an architect, listened to her client. Hearst was describing the vacation home he wanted her to design. It would be on his property along the Pacific Ocean in California.

Hearst told Morgan he wanted the home to be "simple."

"Simple," Morgan thought, imagining a basic design.

Julia Morgan was California's first female architect. When Julia met with Hearst on that day in 1919, she had already designed many buildings. Julia was known for working closely with clients.

Julia soon discovered what kind of home Hearst really had in mind. He was a rich man who often traveled around the world. He wanted a house where he could display his artworks. The vacation home wouldn't be "simple." It would be a massive museum!

Julia drew up plans for a castle-like house. She also designed three huge guest houses. During construction, Julia checked to make sure workers were building everything right. She worked on every little detail.

Hearst liked to attend to every detail, too. He was also used to having things his way. He once told Julia to rip out a fireplace and move it. Later, he told her to move it back. Hearst also gathered more art treasures. Julia had to design spaces for them.

One treasure that Hearst found was part of a Roman temple. First, he wanted Julia to place the temple in a garden, then by a pond. Julia sketched ideas and he kept changing them. Later, Julia designed an outdoor pool. Hearst asked her to enlarge and rebuild it several times. At one end of the new pool, they placed the Roman temple!

Today, the property is open to the public. It's known as Hearst Castle. Tourists from around the world come to see Hearst Castle. Julia Morgan spent over 20 years designing— and redesigning it.

The main house at the estate, called Hearst Castle

Nonfiction Reading Practice, Grade 4 • EMC 3315 • ©2003 by Evan-Moor Corp.

Name _____

Designing Hearst Castle

Fill in the bubble to answer each question or complete each sentence.

1. Julia Morgan was California's first female _____.
   - Ⓐ publisher
   - Ⓑ engineer
   - Ⓒ designer
   - Ⓓ architect

2. Which word does <u>not</u> describe Hearst's vacation home?
   - Ⓐ palace
   - Ⓑ cottage
   - Ⓒ mansion
   - Ⓓ castle

3. Why did Hearst's vacation home become a "massive museum"?
   - Ⓐ Hearst traveled a lot.
   - Ⓑ Hearst was picky and choosy.
   - Ⓒ Hearst wanted to show off his treasures.
   - Ⓓ Hearst's family kept growing larger.

4. Why did Julia often visit the property while the vacation home was being built?
   - Ⓐ She wanted to make sure the workers were building everything right.
   - Ⓑ She liked to see the ocean.
   - Ⓒ She brought her treasures to the home.
   - Ⓓ She kept taking visitors there.

5. *Patient* is a good word to describe _____.
   - Ⓐ William Randolph Hearst
   - Ⓑ Julia Morgan's clients
   - Ⓒ Julia Morgan
   - Ⓓ the wealthy publisher

Bonus: On the back of this page, write three sentences explaining how you would feel if you were an architect who worked for a client like Hearst.

Reaching a Goal

"Designing a building is exciting," Julia Morgan explained. "I can work out the details in my mind, like a composer writing a symphony! That's why I want to be an architect!"

Julia's father stared at his nineteen-year-old daughter. "An architect?"

Her mother stood up and clapped. "I think you'd make a fine architect, Julia!"

That was back in the early 1890s. Few women were architects then. But Julia Morgan was determined to reach her goal.

Julia was already taking classes at the University of California, Berkeley. But it had no school for architects. So she studied engineering there. Julia was the only woman in all her engineering classes. In 1894, Julia graduated. She was the first woman to receive an engineering degree at Berkeley.

Julia was still interested in architecture. A teacher at Berkeley told Julia about a fine architecture school. It was in Paris, France.

In 1896, Julia traveled to Paris. When she arrived, the school wouldn't accept her. No woman had ever studied architecture there. Julia didn't give up. Students had to pass a difficult test to get into the school. She decided to stay in Paris and study for it. Julia studied and worked as an apprentice for an architect. She learned the basics of architecture from the master architect. Julia also spent time traveling and drawing pictures of buildings.

Finally, Julia was allowed to take the test. She did well, but her test was graded much harder than the men who took the test. Disappointed, she returned to work as an apprentice. Six months later, she took the test again. This time she scored near the top of her class. The college had to admit her now. Four years later, she became the first woman to receive a degree in architecture from that famous school.

Julia returned home. In 1904, she took a test and became the first woman in California to get an architect's license. She had finally reached her goal!

Julia designed over 700 buildings during the next 47 years. Her great successes helped encourage many women to become architects.

Julia Morgan during her college years

Nonfiction Reading Practice, Grade 4 • EMC 3315 • ©2003 by Evan-Moor Corp.

Name _____

Reaching a Goal

Fill in the bubble to answer each question or complete each sentence.

1. What was Julia Morgan's goal in life?
   - Ⓐ She wanted to go to many colleges.
   - Ⓑ She wanted to become an architect.
   - Ⓒ She wanted to travel to Paris.
   - Ⓓ She wanted to please her parents.

2. Why did Julia Morgan not study architecture at Berkeley?
   - Ⓐ She wanted to be the first woman to get an engineering degree there.
   - Ⓑ She wanted to first learn all she could about architecture.
   - Ⓒ Berkeley didn't have a school for architects.
   - Ⓓ She preferred to study architecture in France.

3. What happened when Julia Morgan first got to Paris?
   - Ⓐ The college wouldn't accept her into the architecture program.
   - Ⓑ She decided to travel for a while, rather than take classes.
   - Ⓒ She got married and read books about architecture.
   - Ⓓ She passed the test.

4. Which group of words best describe Julia Morgan?
   - Ⓐ fine, happy, lucky
   - Ⓑ discouraged, disappointed, difficult
   - Ⓒ interesting, nice, pretty
   - Ⓓ intelligent, determined, successful

5. Julia Morgan's great successes helped encourage _____.
   - Ⓐ young people to go to school
   - Ⓑ men to become architects
   - Ⓒ other women to become architects
   - Ⓓ people to travel to other countries

Bonus: On the back of this page, describe at least three challenges Julia Morgan had to face during the years she was trying to become an architect.

Name _____

Write the important details of the famous person's life.

Who

Where

Sketch

Where (he/she lives or lived)

_____
_____
_____
_____
_____
_____

What (he/she does or did)

_____
_____
_____
_____
_____
_____

Why (it is important to know about him/her)

_____
_____
_____
_____
_____
_____

Name _____

KWL Chart

Before reading the article, write what you already know about the topic. Write what you want to know about the topic. After you finish reading the article, write what you learned about the topic.

Topic:		
K	**W**	**L**
What I **K**now	What I **W**ant to Know	What I **L**earned

Name _____

Making an Outline

As you read the article, take notes on three important main ideas or subtopics.
After you have read the article, write the title of the article. Write three subtopics as
main headings (I–III) in the outline. Write each subtopic's details (A–C) in the outline.

_____
Title of article

I. _____

    A. _____

    B. _____

    C. _____

II. _____

    A. _____

    B. _____

    C. _____

III. _____

    A. _____

    B. _____

    C. _____

Name _____

Multisection Web

Use this web to write the main idea and supporting details for three important paragraphs in the article.

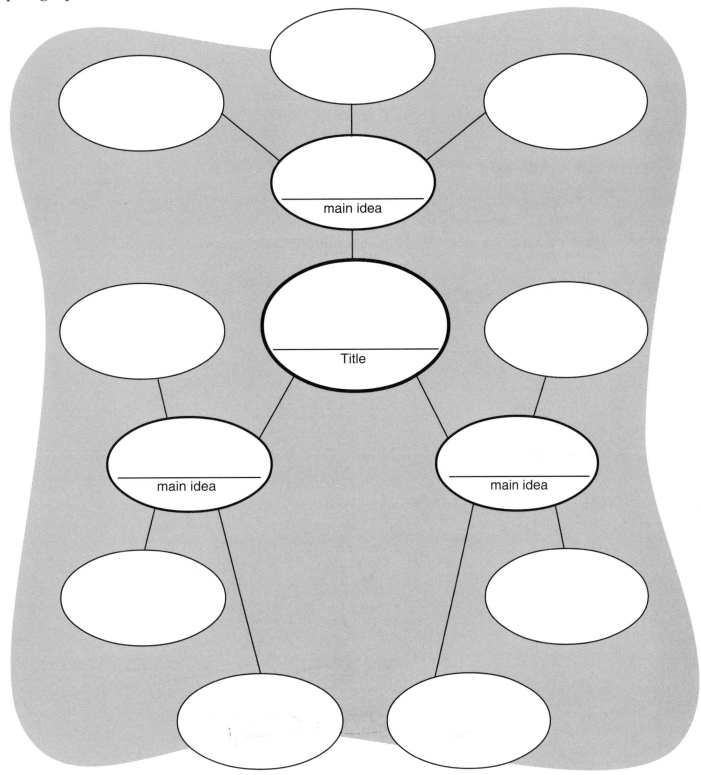

Nonfiction Reading Practice, Grade 4 • EMC 3315 • ©2003 by Evan-Moor Corp.

Name _____

Sequence Chart

Use this chart to sequence the events in the article.

Name _____

Vocabulary Quilt

As you read the article, write new words and their meanings in the quilt squares.

Word: _____

Word: _____

Word: _____

Word: _____

Word: _____

Word: _____

Nonfiction Reading Practice, Grade 4 • EMC 3315 • ©2003 by Evan-Moor Corp.

Answer Key

page 9
1. C
2. A
3. B
4. D
5. C
Bonus: Answers will vary, but should include that the sculpture shows four famous presidents and that the sculpture is so huge.

page 11
1. A
2. C
3. A
4. D
5. B
Bonus: Answers will vary, but should emphasize that more people from many more places know the presidents than the heroes of the West.

page 13
1. C
2. A
3. D
4. C
5. B
Bonus: Answers will vary, but should include that the memorial was made to honor the Sioux Nation and Chief Crazy Horse.

page 17
1. D
2. B
3. C
4. B
5. C
Bonus: Students should mention that there are two senators from each state. (50 states x 2 senators = 100 senators)

page 19
1. A
2. B
3. C
4. D
5. A
Bonus: Answers will vary, but students should say that the people who believed in each plan at least got part of what they wanted.

page 21
1. A
2. D
3. B
4. B
5. D
Bonus: Answers will vary, but should include the idea that people need to actively participate in their government and have a say in how it is run.

page 25
1. B
2. D
3. B
4. A
5. C
Bonus: Answers will vary, but pictures might be of people riding in boats, making moccasins, building forts, and climbing mountains. Pictures of the kinds of animals seen could also be included.

page 27
1. A
2. B
3. D
4. C
5. D
Bonus: Answers will vary, but should describe two ways the Native Americans helped Lewis and Clark. Ideas may include that they gave the explorers food and horses, served as guides, and showed a way to get through the Rocky Mountains.

page 29
1. C
2. A
3. B
4. A
5. C
Bonus: Answers should include three reasons: Jefferson wanted to know about the Louisiana Territory, lands west of the Rocky Mountains, and if there was a waterway to the Pacific Coast.

page 33
1. C
2. A
3. B
4. A
5. D
Bonus: Answers will vary, but should say that the Confederate States were in the South, where there were many large farms. They thought it should be OK to have slaves to work the farms.

Nonfiction Reading Practice, Grade 4 • EMC 3315 • ©2003 by Evan-Moor Corp.

page 35
1. D
2. B
3. A
4. B
5. D
Bonus: Answers will vary, but should explain that Lincoln meant when a country can't agree on something important, it won't last. When he said a "house," Lincoln actually meant the country.

page 37
1. D
2. A
3. C
4. C
5. B
Bonus: Answers will vary, but should say that the Civil War divided the country. It caused much bloodshed. But the war helped end slavery in the U.S.

page 41
1. D
2. B
3. C
4. C
5. A
Bonus: Answers will vary, but will probably include at least one continent and one ocean.

page 43
1. D
2. B
3. C
4. A
5. B
Bonus: Answers will vary, but should include the idea that there was one giant continent called Pangaea, about 250 million years ago, and that it started drifting apart to form the seven continents we have today.

page 45
1. A
2. D
3. A
4. C
5. B
Bonus: Answers will vary, but should include information about plates, that plates float, and that there are heat currents.

page 49
1. C
2. A
3. D
4. A
5. C
Bonus: Answers will vary, but should say that the filament heats up and glows.

page 51
1. B
2. C
3. B
4. D
5. A
Bonus: Answers will vary, but should say that power plants make electricity that everyone uses.

page 53
1. B
2. A
3. C
4. A
5. D
Bonus: Answers will vary, but should explain that hydroelectric plants use rushing water to make electricity, and coal-fired power plants and nuclear power plants use steam.

page 57
1. C
2. A
3. D
4. B
5. C
Bonus: Answers will vary, but might include eye color, hair color, skin color, eye shape, type of hair, and height.

page 59
1. C
2. A
3. B
4. B
5. D
Bonus: Half from each parent: 23 from mother and 23 from father.

page 61
1. A
2. C
3. B
4. D
5. B

Bonus: Answers will vary, but might include that Mendel probably didn't know about chromosomes because they were named and discovered later. Mendel only looked at the pea plants themselves; he didn't have a microscope to study the cells.

page 65
1. C
2. B
3. A
4. B
5. D
Bonus: Answers will vary, but might include the three reasons given in the article. Families won't picnic if it's too stormy, pilots can't fly if it's too stormy, and cities need to be ready if tornadoes come.

page 67
1. A
2. D
3. C
4. B
5. C
Bonus: Answers will vary, but might include information about the wind, sun, clouds, rain, and snow.

page 69
1. D
2. B
3. A
4. C
5. D
Bonus: Answers will vary, but could include a thermometer, hygrometer, wind vane, anemometer, computer, weather radar, or weather satellite.

page 73
1. B
2. D
3. C
4. A
5. B
Bonus: Answers will vary, but should include the idea that the Internet connected computers in different places so they could share information.

page 75
1. C
2. D
3. C
4. A
5. B

Bonus: Answers will vary, but might include sending and getting information, sending and getting e-mails, listening to music, shopping online, and playing games.

page 77
1. B
2. C
3. A
4. D
5. B
Bonus: Answers will vary, but might include the fact that many people, including government workers, can communicate by computer and share information from anywhere in the world.

page 81
1. C
2. A
3. B
4. B
5. C
Bonus: Answers will vary, but will probably say that she was a good student, a scientist, she worked in labs, she discovered two new substances, and she earned awards.

page 83
1. B
2. A
3. C
4. D
5. C
Bonus: Answers should include that she was the first woman to receive a Nobel Prize, she was the first person to receive two Nobel Prizes, and she was the first woman to teach at Sorbonne University.

page 85
1. D
2. A
3. C
4. B
5. D
Bonus: Answers will vary, but could include that she worked hard in college, got two college degrees, made important discoveries about radioactivity, discovered two new elements, won two Nobel Prizes, and was director of the Radium Institute where scientists studied ways to treat cancer.

page 89
1. C
2. D
3. B
4. A
5. B

Bonus: Answers will vary, but might include that dentists help take care of your teeth, they clean and check them, and they fix teeth when needed.

page 91
1. D
2. B
3. A
4. D
5. C

Bonus: Answers will vary, but will probably say that brushing removes food and germs and prevents cavities.

page 93
1. B
2. B
3. D
4. A
5. C

Bonus: Answers will vary, but students might say that brushing removes bacteria and food, keeps teeth healthy, and prevents cavities.

page 97
1. C
2. B
3. D
4. A
5. C

Bonus: Answers will vary, but should say that Anna learned that accidents can happen even on short car trips and that it's important to wear a seat belt to prevent getting hurt.

page 99
1. D
2. C
3. B
4. C
5. A

Bonus: Answers will vary, but should say that seat belts hold people in their seat inside the car, which is the safest place to be in a crash.

page 101
1. A
2. D
3. C
4. B
5. D

Bonus: Answers will vary, but should explain the idea that once a passenger is moving in a car, she keeps moving. If the car stops, and she isn't wearing a seat belt, she'll continue moving inside the car. The laws of physics are natural laws that cannot be broken—unlike the laws that people make.

page 105
1. A
2. C
3. D
4. A
5. B

Bonus: Answers will vary, but should mention that Dr. Charles Richard Drew set up blood banks and researched blood plasma.

page 107
1. C
2. A
3. B
4. C
5. D

Bonus: Answers will vary, but should mention that without dried plasma that could be mixed with water and given in a transfusion, wounded soldiers might have died.

page 109
1. A
2. D
3. B
4. C
5. D

Bonus: Answers will vary, but might include the following: He went to college, even when few colleges accepted blacks. He followed his dream and became a doctor rather than an athlete. He earned two college degrees. He helped provide much-needed blood plasma to soldiers during World War II.

page 113
1. A
2. B
3. B
4. D
5. C

Bonus: Students should include a picture and a label. Columns are vertical posts, and beams are horizontal.

page 115
1. D
2. C
3. D
4. A
5. B

Bonus: Answers will vary, but should say it's a good thing that she loves math because she has to work so many math problems when she does engineering.

page 117
1. B
2. A
3. C
4. D
5. A

Bonus: Answers will vary, but should mention safety and that the building needs to last a long time.

page 121
1. D
2. B
3. C
4. B
5. A

Bonus: The students should recognize that the chance of landing on heads (1/2) is the same as landing on tails (1/2). Both teams have an equal chance of calling the correct side.

page 123
1. C
2. D
3. A
4. B
5. D

Bonus: Students should recognize that a spinner with all shaded spaces, like Spinner E, gives you the greatest chance of landing on a shaded space.

page 125
1. B
2. A
3. D
4. A
5. C

Bonus: Answers will vary, but should be similar to the ones shown below the probability number line.

page 129
1. D
2. A
3. C
4. D
5. B

Bonus: Answers will vary, but might say they would buy something with it, save it, or give it away to someone.

page 131
1. C
2. A
3. D
4. B
5. D

Bonus: Answers will vary, but should mainly say the shareholder wants to make money.

page 133
1. D
2. C
3. A
4. B
5. D

Bonus: Answers will vary, but should state that they need money from their shareholders to help run the corporations.

page 137
1. B
2. A
3. C
4. D
5. B

Bonus: Answers will vary, but should explain that Beethoven heard the music in his mind, not with his ears.

page 139
1. C
2. B
3. D
4. A
5. B

Bonus: Answers will vary, but might say that he loved music a lot.

page 141
1. A
2. B
3. C
4. B
5. D

Bonus: Answers will vary, but might say that they would feel sad, frustrated, and angry about not being able to hear. They might also say they'd feel happy that they could still write music and play music anyway.

page 145
1. B
2. C
3. A
4. B
5. D

Bonus: Answers will vary, but students should explain that looking at objects helps artists draw the details needed to make drawings look realistic.